The Preacher's Bible Guide

Understanding the Scriptures Without Tears

DR. JOHN ONYEKACHI MADU

LitPrime Solutions
East Brunswick Office Evolution
1 Tower Center Boulevard, Ste 1510
East Brunswick, NJ 08816
www.litprime.com
Phone: 1-800-981-9893

Unless otherwise indicated, Scripture quotations in this publication are from the Holy Bible, King James Version (KJV).

Published by LitPrime Solutions: 11/08/2024

ISBN: 979-8-88703-400-3(sc)
ISBN: 979-8-88703-401-0(e)

Library of Congress Control Number: 2024916753

The Preacher's Bible Guide

Understanding the Scriptures Without Tears

Prepared for Sunday school teachers, deacons and deaconesses, teaching elders, Bible students, and busy called gospel ministers

John Onyekachi Madu

TABLE OF CONTENTS

The book is dedicated to the Eternal Godhead.

Acknowledgements

My special thanks go to my dearly beloved mother, Madam Theresa Anyahuru Madu, who instilled in me an early love and respect for God. Her gracious godly life and traits were able to plant me into loving God and His Word. She has been my model in my walk with the Lord.

My profound gratitude goes to my wife, Evangelist Ruth Madu. Her contribution to this book is immeasurable. I am so grateful to Miracle, John (Junior), and Goodness, my blessed children, whose patience have immensely contributed to bringing the work to fruition.

My sincere gratitude goes to Brother Yoseph Assefa; his wife, Mekdes; and their children. They are true family friends whose heart for God is without guile.

I wish to appreciate my brother, Mr. Peter M. Madu; his wife, Evangelist Augusta; and their children for their support.

Lastly, I would like to express my gratitude to Pastor Ola Popoola, the regional pastor of Deeper Life Bible Church, Ireland Region, and his family for their moral encouragement.

Preface

The English term *bible* is from the Latin and Greek word *biblia* and has the literal meaning of "scroll" and came to be used as "book." The Holy Bible contains an "old" testament and a "new" testament and was written in three major languages: Hebrew, Aramaic, and Greek. Hebrew was the language of the Jews; Aramaic was a widely used language in the Middle East; Greek was a popular language during the Lord's ministry. However, some parts of Daniel and Ezra were written in the Syriac language (Jeremiah 10:11; Ezra 4:8–6:18, 7:26; Daniel 2:4–7:8).

It is so essential to read and perceive the Christian Scripture, since the Scripture is the way God promised to talk to us. In the Scripture, God tells us how we can stay in relationship with him through Jesus Christ. He makes this clear because a relationship with God is all that we need. As a matter of fact, it is a book that is vital; it is a personal letter to humankind that retains an accurate record of the creator of heaven and earth, the almighty God who has proved his infinite goodness for his creation. He revealed himself and his program for humankind's salvation, a programme necessary because of humankind's rebellion. Despite that rebellion, God fulfilled that programme through his only Son, the Saviour of the world, Jesus Christ the righteous (1 John 2:1). After his departure (return to heaven), he sent the comforter as guide to the gospel's recipients to both Jews and Gentiles as promised.

This book is a companion that will serve as a guide through life's journey, a light provided to show us the true way we should go in this dark generation. This guide from heaven is here to give us prophecy on the events of the last day; it is a map to help us enter heaven, home of the saints. What a glorious book! Read it slowly with your mouth. Read it often with your mind. Read the Bible prayerfully. Make sure you know it in your head. Stow it in your heart. Do show it in your life daily. Sow it in the world through evangelism or one-to-one witness to people about the messiah. Most of all, obey it. The Bible is a great library and treasure that requires a guide such as the one in your hand.

Eighteenth-century French writer and philosopher Voltaire did not believe in God; instead, he fought God by all means. He said that within one hundred years of his era, Christianity, along with its sacred book—the Bible—would be wiped out of existence and would be remembered no more. Fortunately, his prediction was unsuccessful; unfortunately, this academician died without trusting God and His Word, the Bible. What a tragedy! Do you know that twenty years after the death of Voltaire, the Geneva Bible Society bought his house for the purpose of printing the same Bible he intended to destroy? It later became Paris headquarters for the British and Foreign Bible Society, which stored and distributed Bibles throughout Europe. Since then many have studied this book and become wise; others believed and are safe from unavoidable dangers. The Bible leaves positive indelible mark in the lives of those who have encountered it.

The Roman emperor Diocletian (AD 245–313) decreed in AD 303 that every Bible should be destroyed. He had been told that, if he could destroy the Bible, he would destroy Christianity because Christians were a people of the Book. Thinking he had achieved his goal Diocletian raised a column with the inscription (in Latin): "The name of Christian is extinguished." He tried to exterminate the Bible, but still it remains the most widely published book in the world today. God's Word is indestructible, and it abides forever (Isaiah 40:8). The Bible stands and is alive. Besides, the Christian Scriptures is the only book whose writer is always present when it is being read and studied. With this and more reasons, I have chosen it even more than anything else in this life.

John Onyekachi Madu

Introduction

There is no mother anywhere in the world who can boldly stand up and claim she has forgotten the date of the birth of her first child, especially when this information is required by the state for the benefit of the child and the entire family's well-being. Dad and Mum know their children's names even in their old age. Schools we attended many years ago, our mortgage payment, the places we've worked—we can't erase these from our memory. Your bank details, whether you have a college degree or not, such as your ATM pin numbers, are all fresh in your mind. Certainly, no one forgets the colour of his or her skin. Such has been my walk with the Lord right from the first day I trusted my life into God's loving care several years ago. To me it remains anew today as it has been during all those years.

Having accepted Jesus as my Lord and Saviour, I instantly became addicted neither to drug, smoking, money, nor alcohol; rather, I became addicted to the Word of God and all things pertaining to godliness. Without noticing the time that passed, I would devote hours to reading and studying the Scripture all in an effort to know Jesus better and learn how to do his will day by day. This was—and still is—in appreciation for what he did for me. Since he first loved me and shed his Son's precious blood on the Calvary cross just for my sake, I decided to love him back.

With consistent devotion and meditation, months after I accepted Jesus, I began a survey of the entire Bible. In the fourth year of my intensive search of Scriptures, I was able to go through the Bible many times with good understanding. Yet each time I picked it up to read, it appeared as if I had never read it the first time. Furthermore, I developed a genuine attitude concerning prayer, and that formed part of my daily meal. Throughout this period, I sincerely sought to obey and do only God's will. While in his vineyard, after a decade of formal and informal Bible training, I realized the blessings that accompany Bible study, the reasons everyone should seek to study it, and the necessity of understanding the Bible. I was moved not to hide this invaluable fact about its great value and benefit.

Perhaps you are among the fortunate ones because you hold this Bible guide. Many years back, I ransacked quite a few good bookshops, searching for a comprehensive guidebook, but, even though there were several good books on the market, I could not find one that could match the wealth of knowledge contained the book you hold in your hands. It will be obvious to the aspiring Bible reader that this book should not be taken as just an academic pursuit of the writer, a way of passing religious examinations, teaching English vocabulary, or just a way to have something to deliver in the pulpit as a preacher or a way of mastering manners and customs of the land of the Bible. Instead, it should be seen as a means of drawing the seeking reader closer to God and to help others to experience the great treasure I have discovered in knowing Jesus Christ. The Scripture holds the answer to the past, present, and future of the humanity. Permit me to call this book "PPP"; that is, pray, pick, and preach. Whether you are a Sunday school teacher, a deacon or deaconess in a local assembly, a teaching elder, a Bible student who has a project to submit, or a busy called gospel minister, it is good for you to have at least a copy for your own bookshelf.

Notwithstanding, be aware that Judaism has twenty-four books; Protestants, sixty-six; Roman Catholics, seventy-three; while the Eastern Orthodox, Coptic, and Ethiopian Christian churches have seventy-eight or more. In this book, attention is particularly given to the Bible that consists of sixty-six books, 1,189 chapters, 31,175 verses, with 3,566,480 letters and 810,697 words in total. Though there are various Bible translations, you absolutely need a good Bible guide like this to direct your steps as you travel from Genesis through Revelation. A note of warning: This book is not another Bible; rather, it is a guide to the Christian sacred book. You can study the Bible as you explore the guide or use the guide as a reference book.

An encouraging feature of the guide is that I have included three cardinal segments that apply to each book of the Bible: The Book, The Contents, and The Statistics. These elements will enable you to properly view and comprehend the intentions of each author. I have also introduced every book of the Bible with additional information: the receiver of the letter, when the text was written, the time of the writing, and why it was written. I have included a substantial and understandable teaching outline in alliteration form. This allows you to read the Scriptures intelligently and spiritually. It is a must-have book for anyone who desires to serve the Lord Christ and is zealous to see spiritual growth in the house of God, the Church. Included at the end of the book are three appendices: Bible Canon, The Gap, and Quotes about the Bible.

Read on and enjoy your Bible.

Part 1: Hebrew Scripture

Hebrew Scripture

The Jewish Bible in Hebrew is known as TaNaK. The acronym TaNaK stands for the three subdivisions: First is Torah, or "law," which comprises the five books of Moses. Second is Nevi'im, or "prophets," historical and prophetical books. Third is Ketuvim, or "writings," which are poetical and wisdom books.

The Old Testament Scripture focuses primarily on the relationship between God and the people of Israel. There are thirty-nine books in the English Bible that contain the terms and conditions of this union. Jews are not pleased when their sacred book is tagged "Old" Testament. They believe the Hebrew Scripture is only one and is without a substitute. Christians, on the other hand, refer it so because, to them, it is just a shadow instead of substance. It represents reality that is yet to come. Believers in Christ hold a belief that the contents of the sacred covenant of the Jews is part of the dealings of God with the entire universe. They view it as a profitable document that is without any error. With this in mind, no Christian denies the Old Testament. It is part of their book, but it has its complete fulfilment in the New Covenant—the New Testament. The Old Testament books are: Genesis, Exodus, Leviticus, Numbers, Deuteronomy, Joshua, Judges, Ruth, 1 and 2 Samuel, 1 and 2 Kings, 1 and 2 Chronicles , Ezra, Nehemiah, Esther, Job, Psalms, Proverbs, Ecclesiastes, Song of Solomon, Isaiah, Jeremiah, Lamentations, Ezekiel, Daniel, Hosea, Joel, Amos, Obadiah, Jonah, Micah, Nahum, Habakkuk, Zephaniah, Haggai, Zechariah, and Malachi.

Chapter 1

The Pentateuch

The first five books of the Bible are called the Pentateuch (Fuentes 1985, 25). In ancient periods, books were in the form of scrolls rather than pages bound into book format. In Greek, scrolls were referred to as *teuchoi* and were kept in containers or boxes. But the Greek term for "five–roll" is *pentateucho* (MacDonald 1995, 23). However, the translation of the Old Testament into Greek is regarded as the *septuagint* (seventy scholars), a version which became necessary because the Jews who were living in Egypt at the time could not understand Hebrew.

These books detail how Israel as a nation was chosen by God so that they could show the rest of the world what he is like. It describes the rituals essential for people to worship him the way he demands. It contains pictures and descriptions of Christ's sacrifices. They also include double numbering of the people in the wilderness, and a repetition of the law was provided for the sake of the new generation, or those born in the desert.

Anglican cleric Griffith Thomas summarized the contents of the Pentateuch thus, as quoted in William MacDonald's book, *Believer's Bible Commentary* (MacDonald 1995, 24):

> The five books of the Pentateuch record the introduction of the Divine religion into the world. Each book gives on phase of God's plan, and together they constitute a real unity. Genesis speaks of the origin of the religion, and of the people chosen by God as its medium. Exodus records the formation of the people into a nation, and the establishment of God's relationship with it. Leviticus shows various ways in which this relationship was maintained. Numbers shows how the people were organized for the purpose of commencing life of the Divine religion in the Promised Land. This book also tells of the nation's failure and consequent delay, with re–organization. Then Deuteronomy shows how the people were prepared, while on the border of the Promised Land, for the entry which was soon to follow.

Genesis

Introduction

The Hebrew appellation of Genesis derives from its opening phrase, *Bereshith*: "In the beginning." Its English title is taken from the Greek name given to the book.

The book of Genesis is the first of the five books of the Bible called the Pentateuch. *Pentateuch* is a Greek term used for the writings of Moses. These five books of law and instruction are traditionally assumed to have been written by Moses, with the exception of a chapter in Deuteronomy that records his death. In Judaism, these five books are known as the Torah, a special word for the Hebrew scriptures and tradition of the Jews (Bowker 1999, 24).

Genesis is correctly placed at the start of the Holy Bible because it informs us of the origin of everything that exists except the beginning of God the Creator. It includes images and phrases which are uniquely displayed but demonstrate apparently an insight of the nature of man's fall (Genesis 3:1–24) and God's first promise to restore humankind to its original purpose by his Son (Genesis 3:15).

The book begins with Adam and Eve in the garden and ends with the sons of Jacob in Egypt. Genesis appeals to everyone, both great and small—servant, master, soldier, civilian, businessperson, student, lawyer, homemaker, even a king. The list is absolutely comprehensive and without end. It answers questions such as: Where did we come from (Genesis 1:1)? Why are we here (Genesis 15:6)? And where are we going (Genesis 25:8)? What a fascinating piece of work! Therefore, it is essential to commence with this book.

The Book

Penman: The book of Genesis does not truly mention any particular individual as owner of this work. We believe the Torah and the early Christian teaching that the writing of Genesis was done by Moses because all the activities in the book are pre-mosaic, and there is no conclusive reason to deny this fact. Besides, the Greek scripture references concern Moses' law (Matthew 19:3–10; Luke 2:22–24).

Person (s) addressed: Though not actually stated, it can be said that the book belongs to the entire universe, including you and me. It is penned for general account purposes.

Period covered: Uncertain. The narratives and other materials come from various times in the history of the chosen nation, Israel, and may have been collected by the early sources. Genesis was written before the exodus; hence, all the events in the book came prior that great event. Given this fact, the date of writing is about 1445 BC.

Position of the book in the Bible: First book

Purpose of the book: The book of Genesis intends to introduce God as the Creator of all life and to keep an accurate record about how everything begins. It never proposes to inform us when God starts to exist since he has neither a beginning nor an ending and shall always be.

Popular people in the book: Adam's family, Enoch, Noah, Joseph, Moses

Places in the book: Garden of Eden, Babylon, Median, Egypt, Luz

Particular events in the book: the creation (Genesis 1:1–31); the fall (Genesis 3:1–24); Noah, God's man (Genesis 6:1–22); the flood (Genesis 7:1–24); Tower of Babel (Genesis 11); son of the promise (Genesis 18:1–33); pure man (Genesis 39:1–23); king's servant's dream (Genesis 40:1–23); Pharaoh's two dreams (Genesis 41:1–57); no Benjamin, no food (Genesis 43); Joseph's cup in Benjamin's sack (Genesis 44); levels of blessing (Genesis 49); last days of Joseph and his brothers (Genesis 50:1–26).

Person of Christ in the book: The Creator (Genesis 1:26)

Portrait of the Book: Law and history

The Contents

I. **Hallowed home, first race chronicled** (Genesis 1:1–2:25)

(a) God's self–existence (Genesis 1:1–2)

(b) God's six days' creation excelled (Genesis 1:3–31)

(c) God's sacred rest established (Genesis 2:1–25)

II. **Human history, fallen race commenced** (Genesis 3:1–11:32)

(a) Wages of wistful served (Genesis 3:1–9:29)

(b) Whole world started (Genesis 10:1–32)

(c) Wiles work somersaulted (Genesis 11:1–32)

III. **Hebrew hallmark favoured race classified** (Genesis 12:1–50:26)

(a) Justification of Abraham through Isaac (Genesis 12:1–26:35)

(b) Jacob and his brother, Esau (Genesis 27:1–36:43)

(c) Joseph's acts till his death (Genesis 37:1–50:26)

The Statistics

There are fifty chapters in Genesis, 1, 533 verses, and 38, 267 words.

Conclusion

God made man the crown of his creation. Humankind disobeyed the Creator irrespective of his loving kindness, and as a result, invoked judgment on all humans. In his infinite mercy, God provided humankind a way of escape by choosing a man through whom the nation of Israel was born, and humankind was restored to the original plight. However, the gracious Lord perfectly made and looks after everything that exists. There is nothing else he expects from man than honour, respect, and worship. Humankind must acknowledge God if they want to enjoy his (the world God created) property. He is God who turns anyone who trusts him into treasure as well as changes us from pagans into priests.

Exodus

Introduction

Exodus means "going out." The book is an account of the people of Israel escaping from slavery in Egypt by the power of God through his servant Moses as his messenger. It chronicles the huge numerical growth of the chosen people during their time of tribulation in Pharaoh's land. It also accounts how God deliberately caused plagues on Egyptians in order to convince the stubborn king to allow these suffering elected individuals to go to their God-given land. On their way home, he gave them his law, which they must obey in order to enjoy their freedom according to the record of the book.

In his estimation and overview of Exodus, Paul Benware explains that, in Genesis 15:13–14, Israel's slavery in the land of Pharaoh is never foreign to the Jewish patriarchs and scriptures. Their years on Egyptian soil are completely God's will for his chosen people. Benware reiterates that Genesis 50:24–26 records the final words of Joseph and his testimony to God's future mighty salvation for these individuals. Joseph's bones significantly become an outward sign that God cannot fail to do all his words (Exodus 13:19; Hebrews 11:22). The message of Deacon Stephen, the first Christian martyr, in Acts 7:20–36 and the account we have in the Hebrews 11:23–29 illustrate some insights and crucial emphasis not seen in the entire book of Exodus (Benware 1993, 51).

Exodus is about the freed people and how they should live their lives as a new people in the new land. This is the second book of the Pentateuch, the first five books of the Jewish scripture. The people moved from prison in Egypt to a palace into the land of Canaan. In a nutshell, it is the book of deliverance.

The Book

Penman: Like the rest of the Pentateuch, we assume Moses was the writer and wrote the book immediately after the completion of the building of the Tabernacle.

Person (s) addressed: The Israelites

Period covered: According to Jewish tradition, the book was written around 1440 BC.

Position of the book in the Bible: Second book

Purpose of the book: The aim of this book is to record a lasting testimony to the nature and work of God. It is account about his redemption of Israel and how she is a peculiar treasure in his sight.

Popular people in the book: Moses, Aaron, Pharaoh

Places in the book: Egypt, Canaan, Sinai, Succoth

Particular events in the book: two Hebrew midwives (Exodus 1:1–22); Moses before Pharaoh (Exodus 7:25–11:10); Pesach celebration (Exodus 12:1–51); crossing of the Red Sea (Exodus

14:1–31); food from heaven (Exodus 16:1–36); Decalogue (Exodus 20:1–26); the Tabernacle (Exodus 40:1–38)

Person of Christ in the book: The Passover Lamb (Exodus 12:46)

Portrait of the book: Law and history

The Contents

I. **The bondage of Israel in Egypt** (Exodus 1:1–14:31)

(a) Moses' birth and his call (Exodus 1:1–4:31)

(b) Moses before Pharaoh and his challenge (Exodus 5:1–11:10)

(c) Moses' brethren leaving for their country (Exodus 12:1–14:31)

II. **The budding journey of Israel's escape** (Exodus 15:1–18:27)

(a) Moses' song of triumph (Exodus 15:1–27)

(b) Moses' people in trial (Exodus 16:1–17:16)

(c) Moses' father-in-law's tribute (Exodus 18:1–27)

III. **The bliss of Israel's exit** (Exodus 19:1–40:38)

(a) Thorough preparation (Exodus 19:1–20:26)

(b) Thoughtful civil laws (Exodus 21:1–24:18)

(c) Total service required (Exodus 25:1–40:38)

The Statistics

There are forty chapters in Exodus, 1, 213 verses, and 32, 692 words.

Conclusion

Irrespective of Israel's pitfalls, the Lord did not slack in his promises to Abraham; instead, he fulfilled his word and through mighty power, set his friend's descendants free. God saved them so that they could serve him. John Philips summaries Exodus in three following words: "life, law, and love" (Philips 2001, 23). We strongly believe God works in miraculous ways. In his greatness, those who put their faith in his awesome power are secured because he is there as their protector; they are his temple. Serve him with your life.

Leviticus

Introduction

The third book of the Pentateuch takes its name from one of the twelve sons of Jacob, Levi, whose family was chosen by God to act as priests and assistants in the tabernacle, the place of his service. Leviticus is a book of devotion.

A respected Bible teacher, John Philips, in his book, *Exploring the Scriptures*, writes about the book: "In Exodus God gets the people out of Egypt. In Leviticus God gets 'Egypt' out of the people. Exodus begins with sinners, Leviticus with saints." (Philips 2001, 25). What a nice and correct remark.

Leviticus can be read along with the book of Hebrews in the New Testament because it contains the shadows of themes, doctrines, and people that fulfilled in the New Testament. Moreover, Moses here got the detailed laws of Leviticus that relate to sacrifices, the priesthood, feast days, and other essential issues. The book teaches that one must be holy to walk with the Lord; it is truly a handbook that should guide Israel as a godly nation.

The Book

Penman: Jesus Himself refers to this book (Leviticus 13:49; Mark 1:44). Despite different views as to authorship nowadays, we still hold to the traditional Jewish and Christian believe that the book of Leviticus was written by Moses.

Person (s) addressed: The Israelites

Period covered: Between 1450 and 1420 BC

Position of the book in the Bible: Third book

Purpose of the book: The book of Leviticus intends: (1) To let God's people understand they are not holy on themselves. (2) That the only way to get to God is to have an obedient heart. (3) All the information the people need to please God is contained in this manual and must be read daily.

Popular people in the book: Moses, the prophet of God; Aaron, the high priest; priests; temple attendants

Places in the book: Land of Israel, place of worship of the People

Particular events in the book: categories of offering (Leviticus 1:1–7:38), ordination of Aaron's sons, (Leviticus 8:1–36), death of Aaron's sons (Leviticus 10:1–20), the atonement (Leviticus 16:1–34), jubilee (Leviticus 25:1–55) vows (Leviticus 27:1–34).

Person of Christ in the book: The Sacrifice Offerings (Leviticus 1:1–7, 38)

Portrait of the book: Law and history

The Contents

I. **The way to God** (Leviticus 1:1–10:20)

(a) Sorts of offerings (Leviticus 1:1–6:7)

(b) Systems of offerings (Leviticus 6:8–7:38)

(c) Sanctity of officers (Leviticus 8:1–10:20)

II. **The walk with God** (Leviticus 11:1–20:27)

(a) Purity towards self (Leviticus 11:1–15:33)

(b) Purity towards God (Leviticus 16:1–17:16)

(c) Purity towards man (Leviticus 18:1–20:27)

III. **The worship of God** (Leviticus 21:1–27:34)

(a) Conduct of the priests (Leviticus 21:1–22:33)

(b) Celebration of the Lord (Leviticus 23:1–44)

(c) Commitment with cautions (Leviticus 24:1–27:34)

The Statistics

There are twenty-seven chapters in Leviticus, 859 verses, and 24, 546 words.

Conclusion

Holiness makes approaching a holy God possible. People should separate themselves from evil and seek after righteousness. Worship of a pure God should never be mechanical. If you follow the rules and patterns recorded in this book of holiness, you certainly will have an apparent way. Walk in it and worship wholeheartedly. It is also a handbook for the temple volunteers.

Numbers

Introduction

The book of numbers covers a period of approximately forty years. The name of the book originated from the dual census of the people of Israel. The first numbering took place at Sinai in the second year after the flight from Egypt, and the second was on the plains of Moab near Jericho in the fortieth year. These years were spent in aimless wandering because of lack of faith. However, the book is interesting and is of a very practical in nature. It tells us of a trip caused by sin and disobedience and that proved the seriousness of the choices we make. Out of that great company that left Egypt, only Joshua and Caleb were allowed to enter Canaan along with the new generation, probably those born in the wilderness. Unbelief is a killer; reject it and live.

The Book

Penman: The book of Numbers was written by Moses near the end of his life.

Person (s) addressed: The Israelites

Period covered: A suitable suggested date is 1405 BC

Position of the book in the Bible: Fourth book

Purpose of the book: The main objective of the book of Numbers is to record the trip of the Israelites from Sinai to Moab during this time period. The writer determines to show that unbelief steals Christians' present enjoyment of salvation. It also stresses God's faithfulness for making Abraham a great nation and fulfilling His promises to him.

Popular people in the book: Moses, Aaron, Miriam, Joshua, Caleb, Korah, Dathan, Abiram, Balaam, Balak, and Phinehas

Places in the book: Mount Sinai, The Wilderness, Kadesh–Barnea, Plains of Moab, Kibroth–hattaavah, Taberah

Particular events in the book: mixed multitude (Numbers 11:4–9), the spies (Numbers13:17–53), Korah's rebellion (Numbers16:1–35), Aaron's rod (Numbers 17:1–11), Moses mistake (Numbers 20:1–13), Balaam and his donkey (Numbers 22:1–41), marriage of female heir (Numbers 36:1–13).

Person of Christ in the book: Star of Jacob (Numbers 24:17)

Portrait of the book: Law and history

The Contents

I. **The pre-planned deals and the trip** (Numbers 1:1–10:10)

(a) Census and roles of Levites (Numbers 1:1–4:49)

(b) Cleansing and various laws (Numbers 5:1– 6:27)

(c) Common practices and legislatives (Numbers 7:1–10:10)

II. **The plains of Moab and the testimony** (Numbers 10:11–19:22)

(a) Setting out of Mount Sinai (Numbers 10:11–36)

(b) Set of Moses' colleagues (Numbers 11:1–12:16)

(c) Spies like Korah and the Levites (Numbers 13:1–19:22)

III. **The people's failure at Kadesh Barnea and the tribes** (Numbers 20:1–36:13)

(a) Practices and events on the journey to Moab (Numbers 20:1–21:35)

(b) Prophet and the new counting on the way (Numbers 22:1–27:23)

(c) Performances (laws) and land of Israel (Numbers 28:1–36:13)

The Statistics

There are thirty-six chapters in Numbers, 1, 288 verses, and 32, 902 words.

Conclusion

All indications are that Numbers is the book of pilgrimage. Two numberings, as I mentioned earlier, are recorded, but do not forget that the people counted at the inception of this book are not the same as those numbered at the close of the book. God punished rebellion. Israel attracted God's stern chastisement for the sin of refusing to go in immediately to have the land freely given to them when they were commanded to do so. Apparently, sin must be punished but can be avoided.

Deuteronomy

Introduction

Deuteronomy is the last book of the Pentateuch. Its English name derives from the Greek word *deuteronomion*, meaning the "second law", which was the repetition of the law written from other books of the Pentateuch. It does not mean Moses received a double Decalogue from God.

The new race was already moving into the land that had been promised to Abraham many years back. Two survivors escaped God's judgment in the desert. In his final speech, Moses drew the attention of these new people and encouraged them to listen to the law of Jehovah before his death. He reiterated that the nation needed to obey the law of God consistently and that Israel's destiny solely depended on doing so. Moses climbed Mount Nebo to view the land of Canaan. He saw it but did not go in just because of unbelief. This is the only book that records Moses' death and burial. His hidden tomb has not been discovered, even today, the reason best known to God. Learn the good part of this great man. Don't worry much about Moses' burial ground as others do; rather, be concerned to do the will of God as he did in His house (Numbers 12:1; Hebrews 3:5).

The Book

Penman: Moses was the writer, except the last chapter, which records his death and may have been written by Joshua. It was written in the wilderness east of Jordan.

Person (s) addressed: The Israelites

Period covered: Written about 1407 BC

Position of the book in the Bible: Fifth book

Purpose of the book: The purpose and message of the book is to inform the new generation that if actually they want to go into the land of Canaan and enjoy it, they must remember their forefathers' actions in the wilderness that brought God's judgment on them; they have to seriously consider their present and as well look to their future by obeying the law of the Lord their God.

Popular people in the book: Moses, Joseph, Caleb

Places in the book: Canaan, Mountain Nebo, Mountain Sinai

Particular events in the book: Moses' burial (Deuteronomy 34:1–12)

Person of Christ in the book: Prophet as Moses (Deuteronomy 18:15)

Portrait of the book: Law and history

The Contents

I. **The preview of the history of Israel** (Deuteronomy 1:1–3:29)

(a) Tour from Horeb to Kadesh (Deuteronomy 1:1–46)

(b) Trip from Kadesh Barnea to Beth–peor (Deuteronomy 2:1–3:17)

(c) True view of victory by the Lord (Deuteronomy 3:18–29)

II. **The priority of holiness in Israel** (Deuteronomy 4:1–11:32)

(a) Exhortation to follow the law (Deuteronomy 4:1–5:33)

(b) Exhortation to obey the Lord (Deuteronomy 6:1–8:20)

(c) Exhortation to live in the land (Deuteronomy 9:1–11:32)

III. **The peculiar days of the hero of Israel** (Deuteronomy 12:1–34:12)

(a) People's property in the land (Deuteronomy 12:1–15:23)

(b) People's perpetuation on the land (Deuteronomy 16:1–30:20)

(c) People's particular man leaving the land (Deuteronomy 31:1–34:12)

The Statistics

There are thirty-four chapters in Deuteronomy, 959 verses, and 28, 461 words.

Conclusion

God did not make humankind like robots. He created each human with a will. Moses witnessed his people reject their original King (God) for this reason. He challenged the new generation to own the land given them by God only through obedience and trust in his Word. Moses reminded the nation of God's faithfulness and the unconditional covenant God made with them. Moses was not a stranger among the people; he knew and properly understood his brethren. He took time to explain the danger of neglecting God's warnings. It was God's absolute entitlement to receive allegiance from humankind in general with no exception.

Chapter 2

Historical Books

The historical books are twelve in number. They simply record the story of the people of God from the era in which they arrived in the land of Canaan to the time they came back from exile. These books detail the conquest of the Promised Land, the constant defeat of the people, as well as their exile in Babylon. There are two major systems of government in these books, democracy and theocracy. The books involved include Joshua, Judges, Ruth, 1 Samuel, 2 Samuel, 1 Kings, 2 Kings, 1 Chronicles, 2 Chronicles, Ezra, Nehemiah, and Esther.

Joshua

Introduction

The Hebrew title is Yehoshua. It means "Jehovah is salvation". The Greek form of the name Joshua is Jesus. Joshua the military leader was chosen by God to take over the leadership of Israel immediately after Moses' death. The book serves as the connecting link between the first five books of Moses and the historical books. It highlights the conquest and occupation by the Israelites under Joshua's military rule. Just as Moses had done, Joshua exhorts Israel to adhere to the Law of God, which God gave them by the hand of Moses. Joshua encouraged the people to obey and to maintain their relationship with God. He was a man of faith and favour, though he failed to produce a leader after him. God is searching for men and women with hearts and faith of Joshua. Will you be the one? We all ought to be anyway.

The Book

Penman: Scholars have different views about the authorship of Joshua. Notwithstanding, Joshua wrote the book because the writing implies that the author was an eyewitness of the events in this book. But the book may have been completed after Joshua's death by Phinehas, his son, and by Eleazer, the high priest at the time.

Person (s) addressed: The Israelites

Period covered: 1400–1350 BC

Position of the book in the Bible: Sixth book

Purpose of the book: The aim of Joshua's writing is to demonstrate the mercy of God and his willingness to reward those who place their confidence and hope in him as seen in the lives of Abraham, Caleb, and Joshua. It is also to record the victory God gave to Israel by taking over the land of Canaan. Finally, the book intends to inform us that, when God called Joshua, Joshua chose to believe and trust the promises of God. He saw waters parted, walls destroyed, the sun standing still, and thirty-one kingdoms conquered. Joshua trusted God's faithfulness.

Popular people in the book: Joshua, Caleb, Rehab, Gibeonites

Places in the book: Cities of the refugees, Gilgal, Jericho

Particular events in the book: harlot rehab (Joshua 2), memorial stones (Joshua 3–4), the fall of Jericho's wall (Joshua 6), the sin of Achan (Joshua 7), the Gibeonites (Joshua 9), Joshua's last word (Joshua 24).

Person of Christ in the book: The captain of the Lord's army (Joshua 5:13–15)

Portrait of the book: History

The Contents

I. **The commission regarding the land** (Joshua 1:1–5:15)

(a) Healthy commentary (Joshua 1:1–18)

(b) Harlot's covenant (Joshua 2:1–24)

(c) Hasty crossing (Joshua 3:1–5:15)

II. **The conquering of the rest of the land** (Joshua 6:1, 12:24)

(a) Central Canaan (Joshua 6:1–8:35)

(b) Southern Canaan (Joshua 9:1–10:43)

(c) Northern Canaan (Joshua 11:1–12:24)

III. **The colonisation and the rampancy of the land** (Joshua 13:1–24:33)

(a) Spoils shared (Joshua 13:1–19:51)

(b) Sacred sites (Joshua 20:1–22:34)

(c) Strategized speech (Joshua 23:1–24:33)

The Statistics

There are twenty-four chapters in Joshua, 685 verses, and 18, 858 words.

Conclusion

Some have believed that Canaan is the same as heaven. It is never true. Joshua and the people had to fight to possess the free land. However, Joshua's subjects defeated their enemies only by the power, strength, and mercy of the Lord God of Israel. The lands of Canaan were distributed among the people. We must all depend and believe God to show his mighty works through us so that we can get what is ours. To achieve it, we must agree with God totally; otherwise, we will lose it. Just act when God clearly has spoken.

Judges

Introduction

The book is named after the thirteen judges of Israel. It covers the time from the death of Joshua to the birth of Samuel, the prophet. It was an unstable time that spanned about 345years. Judges is just the opposite of the book of Joshua. The book of Judges is the book of defeat while Joshua is a book of victory. You will notice in this book a series of rebellion, punishment, repentance, and deliverance. It records the experiences of the people of Israel during the period of theocracy. The book closes with sad news. Obviously, God needs our cooperation to bring all to an expected end.

The Book

Penman: 1 Samuel 10:25 supports Samuel the prophet as the author.

Person (s) addressed: The Israelites

Period covered: The book of Judges is best dated in the first half century of the rule of monarchy between 1050–1000 BC. This is because of the repeated phrase in the following passages of the Scripture: Judges 17:6; 18:1; 19:1; and 21:25. These passages suggest there was no king when the book was written. Again, Judges1:21 indicates that the original inhabitants at the period (the Jebusites) had not finally left Jerusalem. In verse 29, Gezer is mentioned. We know that Pharaoh gave King Solomon Gezer as a wedding gift later.

Position of the book in the Bible: Seventh book

Purpose of the book: The book intends to expose man's lost nature and his need for a saviour. It reveals the instability and inconsistency of the people of Israel in their relationship with God. It also reveals God's mercy and patience towards his people.

Popular people in the book: Samson; Delilah; Gideon; Jephthah; Deborah, Ehud, a left-handed man; Othniel, the younger brother of Caleb

Places in the book: Canaan, Zidon, Moab, Ammon, Mesopotamia

Particular events in the book: Prophetess Deborah (Judges 5), Jephthah's daughter (Judges 11), Samson's wife (Judges 14), Samson and Delilah (Judges 16), Micah's idolatry (Judges 17–18), The Levites' concubine and wives given to the Tribe of Benjamin (Judges 19–21).

Person of Christ in the book: The Angel of the Lord (Judges 2:15)

Portrait of the book: History

The Contents

I. **The period of Israel's open disobedience** (Judges 1:1–3:6)

(a) Judah's strength fortified (Judges 1:1–18)

(b) Failure of Joseph's house (Judges 1:19–36)

(c) Joshua's absence felt (Judges 2:1–3:6)

II. **The period of Israel's judges' demonstrations** (Judges 3:7–16:31)

(a) Saviours were sent (Judges 3:7–15:20)

(b) Samson's great strength (Judges 16:1–21)

(c) Strong man sleeps (Judges 16:22–31)

III. **The period of Israel's moral decadence** (Judges 17:1–21:25)

(a) Micah and Dan's idolatrous practice (Judges 17:1–18:31)

(b) Months of lifeless and men of the city (Judges 19:1–30)

(c) Men of Benjamin's abomination and results (20:1–21:25)

The Statistics

There are twenty-one chapters in Judges, 618 verses, and 18, 976 words.

Conclusion

Judges is full of man's failures and God's constant mercy and grace. Sin will always be punished; it is so contagious. Sin demotes, disgraces, and destroys. Yet God forgives a truly repentant sinner. Sin must be avoided at all cost.

Ruth

Introduction

Book of Ruth is totally a book of redemption. It tells the beautiful story of a Moabite widow whose devotion to her widowed mother-in-law, Naomi, led her to marry a godly Hebrew man, Boaz. God rewarded Ruth's honesty and sincerity, and she became the great grandmother of Israel's most loving king, David. Through David's line, the Messiah was born. It is one of the two books in the entire Bible in which a woman is the cardinal character.

The Book

Penman: The author is unknown. Jewish tradition suggests Samuel as the writer. Since the book ends with King David, the book can't have been written before his era. Remember Prophet Samuel anointed David. It is interesting to see that a Gentile woman became one of the ancestors of Jesus Christ.

Person (s) addressed: Israel

Period covered: Probably written during or after the rule of David, 1011– 975 BC.

Position of the book in the Bible: Eighth book

Purpose of the book: This book intends to reveal that there were still some among people who feared the Lord during the period of theocracy, even when Israel went far away from her lover, God. Ruth shows us how God took time to prepare, protect, and preserve a family line of King David through whom the Messiah came.

Popular people in the book: Ruth, Naomi, Boaz, Orpah, Elimelech

Places in the book: Bethlehem, Moab, Jerusalem

Particular events in the book: Ruth clave but Orpah kissed (Ruth 1:6–18), Ruth received a full reward and Boaz took knowledge of her (Ruth 2:1–23), Naomi's godly plan for Ruth (Ruth 3:1–18), union blessed with a child (Ruth 4:1–22).

Person of Christ in the book: Kinsman Redeemer (Ruth 4:14)

Portrait of the book: History

The Contents

I. **Famine in the house of bread** (Ruth 1:1–22)

(a) Life in the time of judges (Ruth 1:1)

(b) Loss in the Nation of Moab (Ruth 1:2–5)

(c) Longing to return home (Ruth 1:6–22)

II. Faithfulness in the heart of the blessed (Ruth 2:23, 3:18)

(a) Ruth's genuine love (Ruth 2:1–23)

(b) Ruth's generous genius obedience (Ruth 3:1–9)

(c) Ruth's grandiose devotion (Ruth 3:10–18)

III. Formation of the godly home of Boaz (Ruth 4:1–22)

(a) The witness (Ruth 4:1–10)

(b) The woman (Ruth 4:11–12)

(c) The wedding (Ruth 4:13–22)

The Statistics

There are four chapters in Ruth, 85 verses, and 2, 578 words.

Conclusion

The book of Ruth proves the non-prejudicial love of God for all races including a Moabite into the family line of the Messiah. It demonstrates and foreshadows Christ's payment for mankind in the loving redemption of Ruth by Boaz. God rewards faithfulness. He loves all people equally and desires them to trust him. God honours nothing else but faith. You are justified through faith not nationality.

1 Samuel

Introduction

The book of 1 Samuel is a transitional book in history of Israel, recording the change in leadership from Judges to Kings. Between the birth of Samuel and the death of Saul there was a period of fifty-five years. The book is all about four men and their weakness. The office of the priest during the days of High Priest Eli and his two sons was discredited messed. Samuel, who was regarded as the best judge in Israel in his time, ended up disgracing his office because of his sons' obnoxious attitudes. Saul, Israel first king and the nation's choice for king, was a complete reproach to himself and his people. Finally, God's choice for king, David, also failed. Think about his conspiracy, adultery, and murder. The effect of his sins shook the whole nation. While we learn from Bible characters, we must look to Jesus as yardstick.

The Book

Penman: Samuel was the writer of this book, though much of the later material was written after the prophet's death.

Person (s) addressed: The Nation of Israel

Period covered: The text gives few clues, but the date of the book is about 1020–900 BC.

Position of the book in the Bible: Ninth book

Purpose of the book: The book intends to document the great change in the national life of Israel from a theocracy to a monarchy system of government. It also accounts the ministries of Saul, David, and Samuel the prophet in particular.

Popular people in the book: Samuel, Saul, Jonathan, David, Eliab, Ahimelech, Hannah, Goliath, Achish, Abiathar, Eli, and Elkanah

Places in the book: Na'ioth in Ra'mah, Shiloh, Tishbe, Ebenezer, Aphek, Shochoh, Valley of Elah, Gath, Nob, Ziklag, Hebron, Mount Gilboa, Jabesh–gilead, Bezek, Gilgal, Wall of Beth– shan

Particular events in the book: family of Elkanah (1 Samuel 1:1–28), Hannah's prayer of praise (1 Samuel 2:1–36), Saul rejected as a king (1 Samuel 15:1–35), David anointed (1 Samuel 16:1–23), Goliath challenges the army of the Lord (1 Samuel 17:1–58), David saves Saul's life (1 Samuel 24:1–22; 26:1–25), Abigail's great wisdom and her marriage with King David (1 Samuel 26:1–25), Saul and the witch at Endor (1 Samuel 28:1–25), Saul's death (1 Samuel 31:1–13).

Person of Christ in the book: The Anointed King (1 Samuel 16:13)

Portrait of the book: History

The Contents

I. **Samuel's role** (1 Samuel 1:1–9:27)

(a) Birth of Samuel (1 Samuel 1:1–2:36)

(b) Bruised high priest (1 Samuel 3:1–7:17)

(c) Benjamin tribe's king (1 Samuel 8:22–9:27)

II. **Saul's rule** (1 Samuel 10:27–15:35)

(a) Man's choice (1 Samuel 10:1–12:25)

(b) Michmash's battle (1 Samuel 13:1–14:52)

(c) Mantle's potent (1 Samuel 15:1–35)

III. **David's rise** (1 Samuel 16:1–31:13)

(a) Anointing of David and his service (1 Samuel 16:1–18:30)

(b) Angry man and his wicked heart's subtlety (1 Samuel 19:1–30:31)

(c) A stubborn king and his sword (1 Samuel 31:1–13)

The Statistics

There are 31 chapters in 1 Samuel, 810 verses, and 25, 061 words.

Conclusion

The book of 1 Samuel ends with Saul, his sons, and his personal armour bearer found dead. It all began with the people's dissatisfaction of God's leadership over them. They opted for a human ruler and got one. The last result was nothing but fatality. Obedience is better than sacrifice. Partial obedience is never obedient. You will either follow God's instructions and obey them or reject them and suffer the consequential aftermath as King Saul did.

2 Samuel

Introduction

It is quite tempting to assume that a certain attainment of victory in life can give us impetus to believe we could break the law of God or take him for granted and get away with it. But this is absolutely ignorance, insensitivity of mind, and lack of respect for the God we claim to have acknowledged. It does not really matter who is involved or the personality of the individual or individuals concerned. Sin will always be sin whether big or small, and it shall never escape or be overlooked. So, sin is punishable.

The book of 2 Samuel gives us an account of David's life in three separate ways; namely, his years of triumphs, his transgressions, and his years of troubles. Finally, it ends with the blessing of Solomon by David, his father.

The Book

Penman: In the original, 1 Samuel and 2 Samuel were a single book. Regardless, the same individual who wrote the first book is assumed to be the author of the second book

Person (s) addressed: Israel's leaders

Period covered: About 1020–900 BC

Position of the book in the Bible: Tenth book

Purpose of the book: The book of 2 Samuel simply records the highlights of the rule of David, Israel's greatest king, and the covenant God made with him.

Popular people in the book: David, Nathan, Absalom, Abner, Joab, Ishbosheth, Phaltiel, Shimei, Michal, Baanah, Rechah, Jonathan, Mephibosheth, Hiram, Ziba, Asahel, Ahithophel, Abishai

Places in the book: Hebron, Bahurim, Gittaim, Jezreel, Mahanaim, Pool in Hebron, Sepulchre of Abner in Hebron, Millo, Valley of Rephaim, Pool of Gibeon, Helkathhazurim, Well of Sirah, Tekoah

Particular events in the book: vain favour-seeking man and David's lamentation (2 Samuel 1:1–27), Abner's death and Joab's multiple curses (2 Samuel 3:17–39), Mephibosheth's receipt of kindness just because of his father (2 Samuel 9:1–13), David's sin (2 Samuel 11:27–12:23), death of Ammon, (2 Samuel 13:1–39), Absalom's conspiracy (2 Samuel 15:1–37), Shimei's curses on the king (2 Samuel 16:1–14), Ahithophel's evil counsel and death (2 Samuel 16:23–18:33), David back in Jerusalem (2 Samuel 19:9–43), Philistines giants destroyed (2 Samuel 21:15–22), Gibeonites' hard demand and God's judgment on David's secret sin (2 Samuel 21:1–14), a list of David's great men (2 Samuel 23:1–39), three options offered to David (2 Samuel 24:1–25).

Person of Christ in the book: The seed of David (2 Samuel 7:12)

Portrait of the book: History

The Contents

I. **The prosperous era of David** (2 Samuel 1:1–10:19)

(a) Sad news of Saul's death announced (2 Samuel 1:1–27)

(b) Security of David definitely assured (2 Samuel 2:1–5:25)

(c) Stable triumphs described accurately (2 Samuel 6:1–10:19)

II. **The privacy era of David** (2 Samuel 11:27–12:31)

(a) A palace adultery viewed (2 Samuel 11:1–13)

(b) A planned murder verified (2 Samuel 11:14–21)

(c) A plain confession verbalized (2 Samuel 12:1–39)

III. **The perilous era of David** (2 Samuel 13:39–24:25)

(a) A house of David (2 Samuel 13:1–14:33)

(b) A heart of David (2 Samuel 15:1–16:14)

(c) A headship of David (2 Samuel 16:15–24:25)

The Statistics

There are twenty-four chapters in 2 Samuel, 695 verses, and 20, 612 words.

Conclusion

At the age of thirty, David became king of Judah; he ruled for forty years. As we look into his life, we may obviously label him a failure due to his moral weakness, especially with women. However, God called him "a man after his own heart". God is the right judge. When God's Spirit controls a person's heart, what follows will be blessing and success. On the other hand, when selfish desires are in charge, the outcome will be retribution and failure. Then we must allow God to control our lives. It is wrong to pretend that nothing serious had happened when his divine order has been violated. When you cross the red line, you must admit to it and not deny it. God is rich in mercy.

1 Kings

Introduction

In the Jewish texts, 1 Kings and 2 Kings are taken as one book. They give us a comprehensive record of the Jewish monarchy from the death of David to the Babylonian exile. When the leadership of King David was about to end, he gave an exclusive advice to his son, Solomon, who was likely to become the successor. The wisest man started well but finished roughly and shamefully because of his strange foreign wives. What we permit into our lives matters, and we will certainly be held responsible.

The Book

Penman: The human writer is not known. Many scholars agree that 1 Kings is compiled from records and by the guidance of the Holy Spirit before the captivity period of Judah, with the last editing taking place during captivity. Some have suggested the following men as authors of the book: Ezekiel, Ezra, and Jeremiah.

Person (s) addressed: The nation of Israel

Period covered: Approximately 560–535 BC

Position of the book in the Bible: Eleventh book

Purpose of the book: The book intends to document in detail the events of the united kingdoms of Israel under King Solomon. It also informs of the divided kingdom under Solomon's son, Rehoboam, whose advisers were young men in lieu of elders.

Popular people in the book: Solomon, Rehoboam, Jeroboam, Elijah, Ahab, Asa, Jehoshaphat, Jezebel

Places in the book: Israel, Judah

Particular events in the book: Adonijah's attempt to claim the throne (1 Kings 1:1–27), Solomon chosen as king in place of his father (1 Kings 2:1–46), New king's request for wisdom and his wise judgment (1 Kings 3:1–28), Solomon's Temple (1 Kings 6:38–7:51), Visit of the queen of Sheba and the king's riches and greatness (1 Kings 10:1–29), King Solomon's enemies and his love for outlandish women (1 Kings 11:1–43), Man of God's death for rebellion (1 Kings 13:1–34), House of Jeroboam (1 Kings 14:1–14), Mount Carmel's contest (1 Kings 18:1–46), Naboth's garden and Ahab's death (21:29–22:53).

Person of Christ in the book: A Still Small Voice (1 Kings 19:12)

Portrait of the book: History

The Contents

I. **The united Kingdom of Israel** (1 Kings 1:53–11:43)

(a) Solomon's anointing (1 Kings 1:1–2:11)

(b) Solomon's golden rule (1 Kings 2:12–10:29)

(c) Solomon's rebellion and demise (1 Kings 11:1–43)

II. **The middle years of the Kingdom of Israel** (1 Kings 12:1–19)

(a) People's demand concerning the taxation ululant (1 Kings 12:1–5)

(b) Princes destructive inexpert counsel turned unbearable (1 Kings 12:6–11)

(c) Problem divides people's total unity (1 Kings 12:12–19)

III. **The divided Kingdom of Israel** (1 Kings 12:20–22:53)

(a) Jeroboam becomes king over ten tribes (1 Kings 12:20–14:30)

(b) Overview tabulation of kings of Judah and Israel (1 Kings 15:1–22:40)

(c) Jehoshaphat's plan for Ophir and his refusal to team up (1 Kings 22:41–53)

The Statistics

There are twenty-two chapters in 1 Kings, 816 verses, and 24, 524 words.

Conclusion

God's people, Israel, were to serve a nation that did not know about God because they had made a wrong and unwise choice. Therefore, the decisions we make at any given time are significant and counts. Decisions can either make us or destroy us. Remember that it is not necessarily how we begin, but how we finish. This is a matter of our future. Despite all of this, God offered the Israelites hope based on their willingness to accept him.

Solomon thoroughly and literally enjoyed the blessing of God. Unfortunately, he later abandoned God and joined himself with strange women who took his eyes off God. He continued his rule until Rehoboam, his son, became his successor and refused to listen to his subjects' simple request. Then the kingdom was torn in two, north and south. No one makes it without the wisdom of God. People like Rehoboam who did not have wisdom need wise counsellors, not just young men without experience. We can't offer another what we certainly don't have. Who is your adviser? Get a godly, mature Christian counsellor by your side.

2 Kings

Introduction

The Israelites had to obey God in order to retain his promise. Failure to comply with him kept them away and could have resulted in absolute disappointment. Throughout the period, the Lord sent his messengers who lived among the people with daily messages of warning to stop the impending coming judgment. Both good and bad kings ruled. They needed to turn back to God.

The Book

Penman: Please see the information about the book of 1 Kings.

Person (s) addressed: Israel

Period covered: Approximately 560–535 BC

Position of the book in the Bible: Twelfth book

Purpose of the Book: The aim was to complete the record of the divided kingdom that began in first book of Kings. It also intended to prove that God was still faithful even though his people were sharply rebuked and disciplined because they ignored all the prophet's warnings.

Popular people in the book: Elijah, Elisha, Hezekiah, Josiah, Jehu, Jeroboam, Manasseh

Places in the book: Israel, Judah, Assyria

Particular events in the book: captains were burned by Elijah's invoked fire from heaven (2 Kings1:1–18), Elisha's hard request and Elijah's chariot and horses of fire (2 kings 2:9–18), Elisha saved a widow and her two sons from creditors (2 kings (4:1–7), a maid in Syrian captain's house (2 Kings 5:1–19), A prophet's servant leaves with a curse instead of blessing (2 Kings 5:19–27), the borrowed axe head (2 Kings 6:1–7), Jezebel's death (2 Kings 9:30–37), the eight years of the young king of Judah (2 Kings 22:20–23:25).

Person of Christ in the book: Rod of Elisha (2 Kings 4:29)

Portrait of the book: History

The Contents

I. **History of the northern kingdom** (2 Kings 1–10)

(a) Messengers and the man Elijah (2 Kings 1:1–18)

(b) Mantle of Elijah and ministry of Elisha (2 Kings 2:1–25)

(c) Message of the king for help, miracles in famine, murdering of Ahab's house, and Baal worshippers envisaged (2 Kings 3:1–10:36)

II. **History of the united Kingdom** (2 Kings 11–17)

(a) Jehoiada's reformation (2 Kings 11:1– 21)

(b) Joash's rule (2 Kings 12:1–21)

(c) Judah's rulers and end of the north (2 Kings 13:1–17:41)

III. **History of Judah, the surviving kingdom** (2 Kings 18–25)

(a) Hezekiah's godly reign (2 Kings 18:1–20:21)

(b) Hezekiah's grandson's role (2 Kings 21:1–26)

(c) Hilkiah, good ruler and ruin (2 Kings 22:1–25:30)

The Statistics

There are twenty-five chapters in 2 Kings, 719 verses, and 23, 532 words.

Conclusion

It is obvious that any nation or individual that rejects God is automatically rejected by him too. A place known as Jerusalem, a city of his choice that bears even his name, was destroyed because his people could not respect and give him honour that was due to him. The reason Israel went into captivity was the cause of Judah's ruin. God is no respecter of persons. Listening to the voice of God and heeding his warning saves and delivers us from all forms of danger. Obedience to his Word is essential and enables us to receive help from Him.

1 Chronicles

Introduction

The book of 1 Chronicles is a compendium of Jewish history that covers the same information presented in the books of Samuel and Kings. Both 1 and 2 Chronicles are documented from a priest's point of view. They contain more detail on the organization of public worship, or the religious ceremonies, of Levites and singers, and of the relationship of kings to the worship of the Lord. The attention of 2 Chronicles is focused on the southern kingdom, Judah, because northern kingdom had no bearing on the development of the worship of God in Jerusalem. However, the book ends with David's son being anointed as Israel's next king.

The Book

Penman: The writer is uncertain, though most scholars and Jewish tradition accept the priest Ezra to be the author.

Person (s) addressed: The Israelites

Period covered: Probably about 450–400 BC

Position of The Book in the Bible: Thirteenth book

Purpose of the book: The captivity of the people of Israel had just ended; they had completed those seventy years of slavery in Babylon as had been predicted by the prophets. Returning to their homeland, they remembered their past. They were unsettled, dissatisfied, and confused about their present and future conditions. Worst of all, their old enemies were still around, the city was ruined, and due to fear, many refused to go back.

The book was intended to help the people realize that God had overlooked their past failures, still cared, and loved them in the present. It also was intended to inform them concerning God's good purpose and the wonderful future he had prepared for them if only they would embrace him in full repentance.

Popular people in the book: Saul, David, Solomon, Jehoshaphat, Asa, Hezekiah

Places in the book: Babylon, Judah

Particular events in the book: Adam to Abraham (1 Chronicles 1:1–43), Israel's family (1 Chronicles 2:1–54), Judah's family (1 Chronicles 4:1–43), Saul's tragedy (1 Chronicles 10:1–14), David became king over all Israel (1 Chronicles 11:1–47), The Ark returned to Jerusalem (1 Chronicles 15:1–29), God and David agreed together (1 Chronicles 17:1–27), Destruction of giants (1 Chronicles 20:1–8), A plan to build God's Temple (1 Chronicles 22:1–19), The division of Levites and priests (1 Chronicles 23:32–24:31), Offering for the Temple project (1 Chronicles 29:1–20), Solomon chosen to replace his father (1 Chron.29:21–30).

Person of Christ in the book: The Lord of Heaven and Earth (1 Chronicles 21:16)

Portrait of the book: History

The Contents

I. **The relationships between the kings of Judah** (1 Chronicles 1–9)

(a) Royal lineage (1 Chronicles 1:1–4, 24, 28, 34:2:1–12; 3:1–24)

(b) Related links (1 Chronicles 1:5–23, 29–33, 35–54; 2:13–55)

(c) Remnant returnees' line (1 Chronicles 4:1–9:44)

II. **The records of King Saul's last journal** (1 Chronicles 10)

(a) Saul and his dead sons (1 Chronicles 10:1–7)

(b) Saul's head and Dagon's sanctuary (1 Chronicles 10:8–10)

(c) Saul and his definite sins (1 Chronicles 10:11–14)

III. **The rule of King David son of Jesse Jocund** (1 Chronicles 11–29)

(a) David's fighting votaries (1 Chronicles 11:1–12:40)

(b) David's fathomable victories (1 Chronicles 13:1–20:8)

(c) David's final vigour (1 Chronicles 21:1–29:30)

The Statistics

There are twenty-nine chapters in 1 Chronicles, 942 verses, and 20, 369 words.

Conclusion

The doings of God are so stupendous that it is far beyond humankind's understanding. I see God as a good father. He did bring back to himself the prodigal sons who had gone astray. For the fact that the Lord of heaven and earth rules over our lives, we are assured of his favour.

2 Chronicles

Introduction

The book of 2 Chronicles specifically addresses the religious condition of the nation at the time it was written rather than its own political affairs or life. The glory of Solomon's Temple was given total attention here. The people witnessed a spiritual awakening and transformation as they were led by King Hezekiah. The book details the ruin of the city of Jerusalem and explains the reason for captivity. Finally, the book comes to a close with the decree of the Persian king, Cyrus, that all Jews should return to their homeland.

The Book

Penman: Ezra had been favourably suggested.

Person (s) addressed: The Nation of Israel

Period covered: Maybe around 450–400 BC

Position of the book in the Bible: Fourteenth book

Purpose of the book: God continued to prove himself faithful to Israel. Without doubt, he kept his arm wide open to welcome repented souls. Moreover, God wanted them to look on him, not actually at the Temple or the city. Above all, God made it abundantly clear that, even though he was a God of mercy and endurance, he couldn't be stopped from executing righteous judgment on culprits.

Popular people in the book: Solomon, Hezekiah, Ahab, Asa, Jehoshaphat, Ahaz, Joash, Queen of Sheba

Places in the book: Jerusalem, Babylon, Assyria, Moab, Edom

Particular events in the book: plea for wisdom (2 Chronicles 1:1–12), Temple dedication (2 Chronicles 6:1–7:22), Cliff of Ziz (2 Chronicles 20:16), sixteen-year-old boy became king (2 Chronicles 26:1–23), rededication of the Temple (2 Chronicles 29:1–36), destruction of Jerusalem (2 Chronicles 36:15–21).

Person of Christ in the book: Ark in the Temple (2 Chronicles 35:3)

Portrait of the book: History

The Contents

I. **The throne of Solomon's height** (2 Chronicles 1–9)

(a) His sacrificial worship and worthiness (2 Chronicles 1:1–7:22)

(b) His supernatural wealth and wisdom (2 Chronicles 8:1–9:28)

(c) His successor's weaknesses and wrongdoings (2 Chronicles 9:29–31)

II. **The time of the sinful southern Hebrews** (2 Chronicles 10:1–36:19)

(a) Sudden result of the separation of the people (2 Chronicles 10:1–11:23)

(b) Summary of the rule of the kings of Judah (2 Chronicles 12:1–36:13)

(c) Sins of people caused their ruin (2 Chronicles 36:14–19)

III. **The testimony of speculative history** (2 Chronicles 36:20–23)

(a) Captives' returnees (2 Chronicles 20)

(b) Complete recollection (2 Chronicles 21)

(c) Cyrus's reinforcement (2 Chronicles 22–23)

The Statistics

There are thirty-six chapters in 2 Chronicles, 822 verses, and 26, 074 words.

Conclusion

God never fails to do that which he promises to do. For David's sake, Solomon was blessed and built a Temple, a place of worship for God. A succession of kings ruled Judah. The majority of them were good, while a few were not. They neglected the law of God. Those who left Babylon for Judah needed encouragement and assurance in the land.

Remember, restored Christians, babes in the Lord, and those who are weak in faith require words of exhortation and grace to help them to keep going and stay strong like those who came back. There is nobody who cannot say he or she does not need encouragement in the Christian faith. All of us want to survive in the face of trials and temptation of today. No one is strong on his or her own.

Ezra

Introduction

Ezra and Nehemiah were combined as one book in the Hebrew Bible, and with Esther, they comprise the post-captivity historical books. Cyrus of Persia took over from King Nebuchadnezzar. When he came into power, Cyrus determined to assist the Jewish people to go back to rebuild the Temple of God of Israel in the city of David. Ezra, the high priest, dedicated the Temple but was not happy with the priests taking foreign women as wives.

However, the book of Ezra is a continuation of the book of Chronicles because it is a story of the return of the captives to Jerusalem to build the Temple again. The Samaritan was not allowed to help in the work, and opposition contributed to the slow progress of the construction. Though it took longer than expected, yet the work of the Temple was finished, and the Temple was dedicated to the Lord. As we read the book of Ezra, don't forget the man Ezra—a humble, obedient, helper, scholar, and priest.

The Book

Penman: Jewish tradition informs that Ezra served among the captives in Babylon as a high priest. It is believed he began the Jewish synagogue worship. He was a committed leader and a useful instrument of God at a critical period in the history of Israel. Although the book is anonymous, still Ezra, definitely, was capable and is called a man of letters. So, we may assume that Ezra was the writer.

Person (s) addressed: The Israelites

Period covered: 450 BC

Position of the book in the Bible: Fifteenth book

Purpose of the book: The book aims to document God's trustworthiness and faithfulness to his promises in bringing the Jewish people back into their land as was promised to Abraham some years before.

Popular people in the book: Ezra; Cyrus; Zerubbabel; Aaron, the chief priest; Nebuchadnezzar

Places in The Book: Persia, Judah, Babylon, Egypt

Particular events in the book: God stirred up the spirit of Cyrus to free the captives (Ezra 1:1–11), the captives who came back with Zerubbabel (Ezra 2:1–70), a great shout of joy and weeping with a loud voice at the same time (Ezra 3:3–13), adversaries' evil letters (Ezra 4:1–24), Governor Sheshbazzar's letter (Ezra 5:1–17), Temple work finished, and dedication of the Temple (Ezra 6:1–22), Artaxerxes approved Ezra's trip with many blessings (Ezra 7:1–28), Ezra ashamed to request for soldiers for his journey (Ezra 8:21–23), Ezra's confession and the people's repentance (Ezra 9:1–10:17), sinners list (Ezra 10:1–44).

Person of Christ in the book: The True Priest (Ezra 7:10)

Portrait of the book: History

The Contents

I. **The return of captives under Zerubbabel** (Ezra 1:1–6:22)

(a) Cyrus's decree penned (Ezra 1:1–11)

(b) Commencing duty pre-informed (Ezra 2:1–3:13)

(c) Counsellors' deception perished (Ezra 4:1–6:22)

II. **The remnant grouped under zealous Ezra** (Ezra 7:1–8:36)

(a) Artaxerxes and his royal law (Ezra 7:1–28)

(b) All accompanied him until landed (Ezra 8:1–14)

(c) Account of his voyage unmistaken loaded (Ezra 8:15–36)

III. **The reformation under zenith Ezra** the priest (Ezra 9:1–10:44)

(a) Confession of guilt (Ezra 9:1–15)

(b) Companions of good (Ezra 10:1–2)

(c) Covenant duly grafted (Ezra 10:3–44)

The Statistics

There are ten chapters in Ezra, 280 verses, and 7, 441 words.

Conclusion

The book of Ezra carries a vital lesson for all Christians. One thing that is obvious is that, with the help of God, individuals can rebuild their lives even after the most tragic experiences. Ezra's early years were spent in disciplined study of the Word of God and in worshipful devotion to the Lord. However, it is never too late to become a devoted and committed follower of Christ as was Ezra the priest. From the life of Ezra, we learn that worship of God is one of the greatest tasks believers can engage in. God watches over us and directs this world and its affairs.

Nehemiah

Introduction

Nehemiah was a man of prayer and fasting! He was a cupbearer to Artaxerxes, the Persian king. The condition of his brethren, the Jews, and the Jerusalem walls moved him to leave Persia for Jerusalem where he later became governor. Some freed captives went along with him. Nehemiah's good and profitable plan of rebuilding the city walls was greatly challenged, yet the discouraging opposition from his enemies and disagreement within his own people could not put a stop to his aim. Instead, the project was finished. More exiles came home and registered as Jewish citizens. There was a reformation in the land, and the people returned to God.

The Book

Penman: Some authors agree that Ezra was the writer of Nehemiah. Others have contested that the writer can't be determined. There were roughly twelve years between the end of Ezra's book and the opening of the book of Nehemiah. It is believed that Nehemiah was born in Persia, though nothing much is said about this man except about his work in Persia and his wall project in Jerusalem. His background was totally unknown. The conclusion is that Nehemiah wrote this book.

Person (s) addressed: The Nation of Israel

Period covered: Approximately 420 BC

Position of the book in the Bible: Sixteenth book

Purpose of the book: The book intends to show God's willingness and enablement to use a faithful, available, and teachable ordinary people to accomplish extraordinary work in his name. It also intends to demonstrate the love of God for his people, to record events about the returnees to the land of their own, and to document the reformation caused by a devoted spiritual leader, Nehemiah.

Popular people in the book: Nehemiah, Sanballat, Tobiah, Ezra, Artaxerxes

Places in the book: Persia, Jerusalem

Particular events in the book: Nehemiah in Jerusalem (Nehemiah 2:1–20), the dedication of the wall and Nehemiah's cautions (Nehemiah 12:27–47), joy in Jerusalem (Nehemiah 13:1–31).

Person of Christ in the book: The Restorer (Nehemiah 10)

Portrait of the book: History

The Contents

I. **Nehemiah's toil of construction** (Nehemiah 1–6)

(a) Concerned for the wall (Nehemiah 1:11–3:32)

(b) Confused foes' worry (Nehemiah 4:1–23)

(c) Comforting forgotten weak (Nehemiah 5:1–6:19)

II. **Nehemiah's type of consecration** (Nehemiah 7–12)

(a) Watchmen and registration (Nehemiah 7:1–73)

(b) Worship and rejoicing (Nehemiah 8:18–11:35)

(c) Wall and rededication (Nehemiah 12:1–47)

III. **Nehemiah's task of consolidation** (Nehemiah 13:1–31)

(a) Mixed multitude and misinformation (Nehemiah 13:1–9)

(b) Ministers maintenance and merchants (Nehemiah 13:10–22)

(c) Married men and mercy (Nehemiah 13:23–31)

The Statistics

There are thirteen chapters in Nehemiah, 406 verses, and 10, 483 words.

Conclusion

The book of Nehemiah is a book for leaders. If you are in a leadership position and maybe looking for a way to get your subjects to join in a task, just go through the book of Nehemiah. Here you will see qualities postulated to accomplish a job that seems impossible to do. So, it is the book to read, study, teach, and preach from. Always agree with God and get committed to him. With the Lord alone, impossibility becomes possible.

Esther

Introduction

Esther was a pretty Jewess from the tribe of Benjamin who lost her parents when she was a tender age. She was adopted by a faithful man, Mordecai, her cousin. Esther, who was also called Hadassah (Esther 2:7, 15, 20), later became king Ahasuerus' wife. Esther did not know she was a Jew at the time (Esther 2:10). Mordecai guided Queen Esther and worked as a gatekeeper for her husband. Haman's hatred of Mordecai led him to plan to destroy all the Jews in the empire, but Esther persuaded the king to frustrate the prime minister's desire.

The book of Esther is worth reading because of its remarkable features. The book is not quoted in the New Testament. It does not mention God's name. You can only read about fasting, not religion. Notwithstanding, we notice spectacular events on God's faithfulness even when his people did not show respect to him. Esther 8:9 is the longest verse in the entire Bible. Therefore, the book contains three significant feasts: the king's (Esther 1:1–12), the queen's (Esther 2:1–17), and the Purim (Esther 9:20–31).

The Book

Penman: Jewish tradition assumes Mordecai may have written this book, though several authors disagree on this view. Some have even suggested Ezra or Nehemiah as authors. One thing is obvious: no matter who wrote it, the fact remains that a Jew who had a good knowledge of Persian customs and accurate information of the palace must be responsible for the writing.

Person (s) addressed: The Jewish people

Period covered: Circa 463–423 BC

Position of the book in the Bible: Seventeenth book

Purpose of the book: The book of Esther is meant to indicate how the Almighty God in his love and goodness cares about his own people then and now.

Popular people in the book: Esther, Ahasuerus, Vashti, Haman, Mordecai, Bigthan, Teresh

Places in the book: Persia, king's gate, king's inner court, palace garden, gallows site in Haman's house

Particular events in the book: Esther replaced Vashti as queen (Esther 2:17), Mordecai's promotion (Esther 6:10–11, 10:2–3), Haman was hanged (Esther 7:10).

Person of Christ in the book: The True Seed of The Jews (Esther 3:1)

Portrait of the book: History

The Contents

I. **The formulation of royal plot of God's people** (Esther 1–3)

(a) Former wife's rejection (Esther 1:1–22)

(b) Foreign woman acceptance (Esther 2:1–23)

(c) Foe's written signage (Esther 3:1–15)

II. **The fight of royal plot of God's people** (Esther 4–5)

(a) Positioned compatriot (Esther 4:1–3)

(b) Personnel's cooperation (Esther 4:4–14)

(c) Petition commended (Esther 4:17:5–14)

III. **The foil of royal plot of God's people** (Esther 6–10)

(a) Book of record and recommendation of Mordecai (Esther 6:1–14)

(b) Banquet of wine and request of the queen (Esther 7:1–10)

(c) Blessing of rejoicing in royal apparel and full rest (Esther 8:1–10:3)

The Statistics

There are ten chapters in Esther, 167 verses, and 5, 637 words

Conclusion

It becomes possible because someone cares. Mordecai, the champion, was concerned about the plight of his fellow Jews in a foreign land. Esther, on her own side, played a noble role and demonstrated real faith after Mordecai's wise counsel. Do you remember Esther's maids and her chamberlains, especially Hatach? They all played important parts in the scenario. We do not see the word *God* mentioned in the whole book, but his hand is frequently felt and seen at work. However, Haman; his wife, Zeresh; and all his friends failed. Fighting believers in Christ by the enemies is like combating God. No one fights God and wins. God is indeed behind the story.

Chapter 3

Poetical Books

There are five books of poetry in the Hebrew Bible. These are also known as wisdom literature. They are poetic in nature, consisting of songs, drama, and proverbs. For instance, Song of Solomon concerns about the meaning of human experience; Job and Ecclesiastes address the inequalities of life, suffering, and the question of good and evil in the universe; Proverbs is concerned with our everyday living; and the book of Psalms particularly deals with worship and the praise of God.

Job

Introduction

The book of Job is one of the poetical books. Others are Psalms, Proverbs, Ecclesiastes, and Song of Solomon. Job is read like play or drama. Some believe that Job may be the oldest book of the Bible; hence, it does not make any reference to the Pentateuch in all its discussions. It appears the man Job lived shortly before God called Abraham. If this is true, Israel as a nation did not exist then, even in promise. It is a lovely, long poem written in a dramatic pattern. People from all works of life—Christians and non-Christians—enjoy its deep thoughts and fantastic style (MacDonald and Farstad 1999, 56).

The book opens in heaven with a conversation between God and Satan in which the latter accuses Job of serving God because he has such a comfortable life. To disprove him, God permits Satan to take away Job's circle of comforts. Therefore, we are given a record of Job's sufferings, debates between him and his friends, and the remedy to his many troubles. God at last restores to Job all he had lost: family, wealth, and health.

The Book

Penman: No one can say for sure who wrote this book.

Person (s) addressed: No particular individuals.

Period covered: We actually do not know the exact period. But it may be as early as the period of the patriarch Abraham, around 2080 BC.

Position of the book in the Bible: Eighteenth book

Purpose of the book: The aim of the book is to reject the common and prevalent concept that all suffering is the direct outcome of wrongdoing or sin in the life of a person who suffers, as well to explain that suffering is not always retribution from God.

Popular people in the book: Job, Job's three friends

Places in the book: Uz, a city northeast of Palestine

Particular events in the book: he was a perfect man (Job 1:1), Job did not sin with his lips (Job 2:9–10), Job pledged to trust God (Job 13:15), man full of trouble (Job 14:1), God blessed the later part of Job's life more than the beginning (Job 42:12–17).

Person of Christ in the book: The Living Redeemer (Job 19:25–26)

Portrait of the book: Poetry

The Contents

I. **Job's disastrous afflictions** (Job 1–2)

(a) Job's life (Job 1:8)

(b) Satan's license (Job 1:9–12)

(c) Joy lost (Job 1:13–2:13)

II. **Job's debates for his afflictions** (Job 3–42:6)

(a) Confusions and critics (Job 3:1–31:40)

(b) Comforters and commentaries (Job 32:1–41:34)

(c) Confessions and compliments (Job 42:1–6)

III. **Job's deliverance from his afflictions** (Job 42:7–17)

(a) His friends rebuked (Job 42:7–9)

(b) His faithfulness rewarded (Job 42:10–15)

(c) His fourth generations remarked (Job 42:16–17)

The Statistics

There are forty-two chapters in Job, 1,070 verses, and 10, 102 words.

Conclusion

Tough times come and go, but tough people remain. Likewise, individuals who have faith in God stay to the end, even in the face of ugly and unbearable circumstances. When God allowed certain situations to come to his child, it didn't mean he had evil intentions or wished to punish; rather, he was seeking to promote him at such a time. That could be a sign that God was taking his beloved to a new level of life. In order for this to occur in our lives, God places us where we can gain new experiences for the new promotion so that we can be able to take charge and be in control when the period is fulfilled. At the beginning, it is never pleasant, but at last the blessing is always doubled. That was the case of Job. His situation at the end of his ordeal was admired and was far better than his situation at the beginning. Besides, Job's story primarily teaches us that suffering or earthly possessions should not be directly related to evil or sin. Sometimes good people suffer, and sometimes bad people prosper. Such is life.

Psalms

Introduction

Psalms is the ancient Jewish songbook. It is a collection of 150 psalms. The Hebrew name of this book is *Sepher Tehillim*, meaning "The Book of Praise". It is a translation of the Greek term *psalmoi*, which means "music on stringed instruments." It's also called the *Psalterium* (Latin for "a collection of songs"), and this term is the basis for the word *psalter*. The full Latin title is *Liber Psalmorum*, "Book of Psalms" (Thomas Nelson Publishers 1990, 161). Messiah is prominent throughout. The king and the kingdom are the theme songs of the book. The key term in the Psalms is hallelujah; that is, "praise the Lord." This has become the saying of believers for all ages.

Bible teacher J. Vernon McGee said, "There is a more complete picture of Him in the Psalms than in the Gospels. The Gospels tell us that He went to the mountain to pray, but the Psalms give us His prayer. The Gospels tell us that He was crucified, but the Psalms tell us what went on in His own heart during the Crucifixion. The Gospels tell us He went back to heaven, but the Psalms begin where the Gospels leave off and show us Christ seated in heaven" (McGee 2017, 206). A good comparison.

This book has blessed the hearts of many down-through the ages. When I have been sick at home, or in the hospital, or when some problem is pressing upon my mind and heart, I find myself always turning to the Psalms. They always bless my heart and life. Apparently, down through the ages, it has been that way. St. Ambrose said, "The Psalms are the voices of the church." Augustine, one of the church fathers said, "They are the epitome of the whole Scripture." Martin Luther said, "They are a little book for all saints." John Calvin said, "They are the anatomy of all parts of the soul." It is the only book that contains every experience of man. The truth of the matter is that it always speaks to our hearts and situations.

Hooker comments of the Psalms, "They are the choice and flower of all things profitable in other books." Donne puts it this way, "The Psalms foretell what I, what any, shall do and suffer and say." Herd calls the Psalms, "A hymnbook for all time." Watts said, "They are the thousand–voiced heart of the church." The place Psalms have held in the lives of God's people testifies to their universality, although they have a peculiar Jewish application. They express the deep feelings of all believing hearts in all ages.

Spurgeon, one of the best preachers ever lived, in his excitement about this book said, "The Book of Psalms instructs us in the use of wings as well as words. It sets us both mounting and singing." According to J. Vernon McGee, "This is the book that may make a skylark out of you instead of some other kind of a bird. This book has been called the epitome and analogy of the soul. It has also been designated as the garden of the Scriptures. Out of 219 quotations of the Old Testament, in the New Testament, 116 of them are from the Psalms. You will see 150 spiritual songs that undoubtedly, at one time, were all set to music" (McGee 2017, 206).

The book was written out of deep emotional experiences and intense feeling of joy and sorrow, despair and triumph, hope and fear, love and hate, peace and unrest. The lows and highs of human experience can be clearly discovered in the psalms. No doubt, Psalms contains a prophetic element, and some of them are purely messianic. As we can see later, the book of Psalms is arranged by type and subject. But the book is organized in an orderly manner. In fact, it has been noted for years that the book of Psalms is organized and correlates to the Pentateuch: Genesis, Exodus, Leviticus, Numbers, and Deuteronomy. However, it is one of the Old Testament books. You should read it for its richness; it makes our hearts sing to the Most, High God.

Penman: Psalms was written by several individuals. Many authors contribute one or more psalms. Seventy-three psalms are ascribed to David, the man after God's heart (Psalms 3–9, 11–32, 34–41, 51–65, 68–70, 86, 101, 103, 108–110, 122, 124, 131, 133, and 138–145. An unknown king referenced in the New Testament (Acts 4:25 and in Hebrews 4:7) is said to have written Psalms 2 and 95. Asaph, a priest who led the service of music, wrote Psalms 50 and 73–83 (Ezra 2:41). Eleven chapters are attributed to the sons of Korah, such as Psalms 42, 44–49, 84, 85, and 87 (Numbers 26:9–11). Two chapters are attributed to Solomon, Israel's most powerful king: Psalms 72 and 127. One Psalm is attributed to Moses, a prince, herdsmen, and deliverer: Psalm 90. One is attributed to Heman, a wise man: Psalm 88 (1 Kings 4:31; 1 Chronicles 15:19). One is attributed to Ethan, a wise man: Psalm 89 (1 Kings 4:31; 1 Chronicles 15:19). Ten of the Psalms have been assigned to Hezekiah, while the remaining thirty-nine "orphan" Psalms are anonymous but may have been written by King David, though tradition attributes them to scribe Ezra.

Person (s) addressed: the Jewish Nation, but various audience under several plights

Period covered: It was written about 1000–750 BC

Position of the book in the Bible: Nineteenth book

Purpose of the book: The cardinal objective of Psalms is to make known the God of Israel, the true way to come to him in worship, and to reveal to humankind how he can walk with him. We can be honest with God and can still express our feelings of fear, disappointment, confusion, and so on. The list is countless.

The Book

Popular people in the book: David; Solomon; Asaph, the priest; sons of Korah

Places in the book: Temple, wilderness

Particular events in the book: a description of the godly (Psalm 1:1–6), kiss the son (Psalm 2:11–12), David's question and answer (Psalm 15:1–5), the Lord is my Shepherd (Psalm 23:1–6), no lack (Psalm 84:11), I shall not die but live (Psalm 118:17), hide his Word (Psalm 119:9–11), except he builds the house (Psalm 127:1), praise the Lord (Psalm 150:1–6).

Person of Christ in the book: The Shepherd (Psalm 23:1)

Portrait of the book: Poetry

The Contents

I. **Part one classification**

(a) Material, instructional psalms (Psalms 1, 5, 7, 10, 12, 14–15, 17, 19, 36–37, 39, 48–50, 51–53, 73, 75, 82, 87, 90, 94, 101, 112, 115, 119, 128, 133, 139)

(b) Messianic psalms (Psalms 2, 8, 16, 22–24, 29, 31, 40–41, 45, 61, 68–69, 102, 110, 118)

(c) Millennial, prophetic psalms (Psalms 46, 72, 89, 97, 110, 118)

II. **Part two classification**

(a) Penitential psalms (Psalms 6, 13, 32, 38, 51, 102, 130, 143)

(b) Prayer and service psalms (Psalms 3, 13, 16–17, 20, 22, 25, 28, 35, 40–41, 43–44, 54– 59, 61, 64, 69, 70–71, 86, 122–123, 140–144)

(c) Pilgrim psalms (Psalms 120–134)

III. **Part three classification**

(a) Hallelujah (thanksgiving) psalms (Psalms 18, 21–22, 28, 30–34, 40, 106, 111–113, 115–117, 135, 66, 68, 92, 97, 100–104, 146–150)

(b) Historical (natural) psalms (Psalms 8, 19, 29, 33, 40, 42, 65, 70, 78, 81, 104–107, 114, 124, 126, 129, 132)

(c) Habitual (experiential and imprecatory) psalms (Psalms 3, 7, 18, 30–31, 34–35, 51–52, 54, 56–60, 63, 69, 83, 109, 120, 139)

Here is another reasonable outline of Psalms:

I. **Book one** (Psalms 1–41) reflects Genesis

II. **Book two** (Psalms 42–72) reflects Exodus

III. **Book three** (Psalms 73–89) reflects Leviticus

IV. **Book four** (Psalms 90–106) reflects Numbers

V. **Book five** (Psalms 107–150) reflects Deuteronomy

The Statistics

There are 150 psalms in the book of Psalms, 2,461 verses, and 43, 743 words.

Conclusion

In the book of Psalms, we regularly see the person of God, his only Son, his Word, his work, and even his people. Everyone who comes across the beautiful work of the psalmists should be inspired, transformed, challenged, and hopeful. This ancient hymnbook is for our use. Find time to use it.

Proverbs
Introduction

Proverbs is a guidebook of sound and useful advice containing wise sayings and instructions on various subjects. Proverbs counsels against visiting prostitutes and being conceited. The book advises readers to allow criticism, save for the future, work hard, be patient, delight in and rely upon God. It was primarily written by King Solomon, presumably when he was in his middle age and his intellectual powers were at their zenith. This book is the finest collection of writings that will encourage young individuals not to fall into grave and expensive errors that some experienced people have fallen into. It is a book of today. The penman deliberately and consciously dealt with the tribulations of life that each of us meets in our day-to-day business. No one is exempted. The book is absolutely a manual for the wise. Wisdom is knowledge in action. Get it.

The Book

Penman: The book was primarily written by David's son, King Solomon (Proverbs 1:1). Others that contributed to the collection were king Lemuel and Agur (see 1 Kings 10:6–9; Proverbs 30:1 and 31:1).

Person (s) addressed: Young people, rulers and kings of Israel

Period covered: Around 700–900 BC

Position of the book in the Bible: Twentieth book

Purpose of the book: Proverbs was written to give people (mostly young people) wisdom, knowledge, understanding, and wise counsel. It intends to bring readers into a disciplined life and to help individuals make wise choices. Above all, it was meant to indicate that life without God is a life without hope, meaning, and eternity.

Popular people in the book: King Solomon, Agur, King Lemuel

Places in the book: Israel

Particular events in the book: commencing of wisdom (Proverbs 1:7), prosperity of fools (Proverbs 1:32), dwell in safety (Proverbs 1:33), God's curse (Proverbs 3:33), liars can't escape (Proverbs 19:5, 9), good name and king's friend (Proverbs 22:1, 11), wine bites and stings (Proverbs 23:31–32), confidence in an unfaithful man in time of trouble (Proverbs 25:19), take good care of your enemy (Proverbs 25:21), wounds of friend and enemy's kiss (Proverbs 27:6), hell and destruction are never full (Proverbs 27:20), no lack (Proverbs 28:27), correct your son (Proverbs 29:17), three things that are never satisfied, yea, four things say not … (30:15–16), king Lemuel mother's helpful counsel (Proverbs 31:1–9), a virtuous woman (Proverbs 31:10–31).

Person of Christ in the book: Wisdom of God (Proverbs chapter 8)

Portrait of the book: Poetry

The Contents

I. **The proverbs of Solomon** (Proverbs 1–29)

(a) Wisdom speaks (Proverbs 1:1–9:18)

(b) Walking safely (Proverbs 10:1–22:16)

(c) Wise sayings (Proverbs 22:17–29:27)

II. **The prophecy of Agur** (Proverbs 30)

(a) God's Word (Proverbs 30:1–9)

(b) Generation's wickedness (Proverbs 30:10–23)

(c) Grave warnings (Proverbs 30:24–33)

III. **The prospect of Lemuel** (Proverbs 31)

(a) Mother's advice adhered to (Proverbs 31:1–9)

(b) Maker's approval acknowledged (Proverbs 31:10)

(c) Model's ageless (agender) attested (Proverbs 31:11–31)

The Statistics

There are thirty-one chapters in Proverbs, 915 verses, and 15, 043 words.

Conclusion

Proverbs reveals that wisdom truly is the attitude that puts the Lord first as humankind's rightful guide. We learn in the book that there are two basic classes of people and that both are identified by their character and chosen ways in life. They are either with God or without him, wise or foolish. But wisdom is the principal thing. Be among the wise. Get wisdom, stay wise and be saved.

Ecclesiastes

Introduction

During this period in history, the preacher was very old, having met disappointments and mistakes with daily practical experiences of carnality of his own life. Some see Ecclesiastes as a pessimistic book and believe there is no reason to assume what might have been or think about a better future than what is onboard. In other words, they consider it as obsolete.

Ecclesiastes, however, is from the Greek term that elucidates the Hebrew *koheleth* or *qoheleth*, which means "preacher". This book is completely part of the inspired Word of God. God permits it to be included in the canon of the Scriptures. Despite debates that surround the book of Ecclesiastes, the book gives us lots of great values and inspired messages. It is a sermon book.

The book closes with a powerful section concerning the meaning of life and its purpose, which is to be inseparable with an obedient and loving relationship with Jehovah God. At all times, God must be our focus and priority. No one will ever enjoy the creation if he or she does not know the Creator. This is the message of the book.

The Book

Penman: The question who wrote this book had been widely debated by scholars. Ecclesiastes must have been written in the later years of Solomon's life. Because of the opening verse of the book and several other passages in the book, it is assumed that Solomon penned the book.

Person (s) addressed: Young people

Period covered: Approximately 931 BC

Position of the book in the Bible: Twenty-first book

Purpose of the book: The book intends to prove to the world at large that no one can truly be satisfied without God. It does not matter who you are or what you have acquired in life. God has a space in our lives and he must occupied it.

Popular people in the book: Solomon

Places in the book: Jerusalem, Israel

Particular events in the book: To everything there is a season, and a time to every purpose under the heaven (Ecclesiastes 3:1–9), be not rash with your mouth … let thy words be few—vow and pay (Ecclesiastes 5:2–7), good name, song and laughter of fools (Ecclesiastes 7:1–6), evil must be punished (Ecclesiastes 8:11), cast thy bread upon waters (Ecclesiastes 11:1), remember now thy creator (Ecclesiastes 12:1–7), hear the conclusion of the whole matter (Ecclesiastes 12:13–14).

Person of Christ in the book: One Shepherd (Ecclesiastes 12:11)

Portrait of the book: Poetry

The Contents

I. **The subject of the preacher** (Ecclesiastes 1:1–11)

(a) Preacher's father (Ecclesiastes 1:1)

(b) Proverb's forward (Ecclesiastes 1:2–6)

(c) Profile's fount (Ecclesiastes 1:7–19)

II. **The sermon of the preacher** (Ecclesiastes 1:20–10:32)

(a) Vanity of riches (Ecclesiastes 1:20–6:35)

(b) Virtuous reproduction (Ecclesiastes 7:1–8:35)

(c) Valedictory and reprobates (Ecclesiastes 9:1–10:32)

III. **The summary of the preacher** (Ecclesiastes 11–12)

(a) Casting of bread (Ecclesiastes 11:1)

(b) Complaints of burden (Ecclesiastes 11:2–10)

(c) Conclusion of basic (Ecclesiastes 12:1–14)

The Statistics

There are twelve chapters in Ecclesiastes, 222 verses, and 5, 584 words.

Conclusion

Solomon, King David's beloved son, tasted and experienced life. He was open in showing his school of thought, for he did attend the school of life. And his summary was that, without God, life is useless and all earthly possessions amount to nothing. Based on this very fact, the outcome of Solomon's learning gave him an insight to the reality of God's presence in every life. He then counsels that we should love, obey, and fear the creator. Isn't that a proper advice? The best!

Song of Solomon

Introduction

It would be more accurate to suggest that the Song of Solomon was written during the early reign of King Solomon before his devotion to the Lord became soiled. He was young and deeply in love at the time. The book is a collection of poems that consist of dialogues between a bride and the groom. The poems describe the meeting of Solomon and the Shulamite woman and continue with descriptions of their courtship and finally their marriage. This has been interpreted as God as the groom and Israel as the bride. Therefore, it is an account of their pleasure, joy, and even hardships they encountered. The relationship between Solomon and the mendicant girl indicates that true love in the context of marital commitment is satisfying, beautiful, and encouraging. The Hebrews sung portions of this book at their annual religious feast of Passover. It is all concerning love.

The Book

Penman: According to the book, Solomon penned it.

Person (s) addressed: Solomon's bride, who was from a poor family of the tribe of Ephraim. They loved each other. Marriage should be enjoyed not endured. If it is not experienced this way, kindly go back to God.

Period covered: Between 960 and 930 BC

Position of the book in the Bible: Twenty-second book

Purpose of the book: The primary aim of this book is to record the joy and purity of physical human love within the boundaries of marriage. Invariably, when a man and a woman are legally joined together as husband and wife, they should find satisfaction in their union. If not, it could be a clear sign that both of them know nothing much about love. They need to learn to love each other unless they have not professed faith in Christ.

Popular people in the book: Solomon, Shulamite girl, daughters of Zion

Places in the book: Jerusalem, country hillside, vineyard at Baal–hamon

Particular events in the book: A time of enjoyment had begun; therefore, Solomon sexually and lovingly expresses his desire (Song of Solomon 7:7–8). What a beautiful moment!

Person of Christ in the book: The Beloved (Song of Solomon 2:16)

Portrait of the book: Dramatic poetry

The Contents

I. **The courtship period** (Song of Solomon 1:1–3:5)

(a) Solomon and his bride (Song of Solomon 1:1–2:17)

(b) The Shulamite woman and her beloved (Song of Solomon 3:1–4)

(c) Shocked by their behaviour (Song of Solomon 3:5)

II. **The wedding plans** (Song of Solomon 3:6–5:1)

(a) Definition of love (Song of Solomon 3:6–11)

(b) Description of love (Song of Solomon 4:1–7)

(c) Demonstration of love (Song of Solomon 4:8–5:1)

III. **The married position** (Song of Solomon 5:2–8:14)

(a) Problem with separation (Song of Solomon 5:2–6:3)

(b) Passion with simplicity (Song of Solomon 6:4–8:5)

(c) Pleasantness of seal (Song of Solomon 8:6–14)

The Statistics

There are eight chapters in Song of Solomon, 117 verses, and 2, 661 words.

Conclusion

As can be seen here, sexuality in a real sense is a perfect gift that comes from God. It is a short means by which we demonstrate our most intimate feelings to the one we promise to love till death separates us. Yet the book is more than merely a physical love lesson. It speaks of and illustrates the kind of love that exists between God and his people, and the love Christ has for the Church. The basic lesson is the sacredness and purity of true love. Sex properly used certainly is a joy and a blessing from God, whereas sex used improperly results in pain, regret, and sorrow according to Scriptures. Men and women cannot have sex unless both of them are legally married, otherwise they are contradicting God's Word. It does not matter what culture or society says. What is essential is what God, who made it says about it. So, it should be God first.

Chapter 4

Prophetical Books

The prophetic era started during the period of Prophet Samuel when Eli and his children failed the priesthood office in Israel. Notwithstanding, the writing prophets did not begin immediately until the kingdom was divided and became two kingdoms.

The works of the writing prophets are divided into two groups, one written by the major prophets and one by the minor prophets. The major prophets are not more vital than the minor prophets; rather, the title is simply used because major prophets have more material than the minor prophets. The prophets lived with and taught God's people during those years of Israel's history. They were God's spokesmen. Their books are prophetic messages from God. These prophets were raised when sin dominated the lives of God's people. The prophets warned people of the consequences of refusing to repent and turning away from God. There are seventeen prophets:

Major prophets: Isaiah, Jeremiah, Lamentations, Ezekiel, Daniel

Minor prophets: Hosea, Joel, Amos, Obadiah, Jonah, Micah, Nahum, Habakkuk, Zephaniah, Haggai, Zechariah, Malachi

Isaiah

Introduction

Jehovah is salvation. This is the meaning of Isaiah. He was a prophet sent to Judah, according to tradition, a cousin of that great King Uzziah. Prophet Isaiah married and fathered children. Isaiah was one of the longest-serving prophets; he lived for almost sixty years and witnessed the rules of different four kings of Judah: Uzziah, Jotham, Ahaz, and Hezekiah.

Isaiah lived when Assyria was in power and saw the country take Israel, the northern kingdom, into slavery. Around 150 years later, the Babylonians did the same to Judah, the southern kingdom. Isaiah was such a great help to King Hezekiah, who was his personal friend and adviser at the time. He had a vivid vision of both Calvary and the millennium kingdom.

Isaiah is one of the most-quoted Old Testament books in the New Testament. It contains the largest number of prophecies about Jesus, the Jewish Messiah. Many Bible students have often called this book the fifth gospel. More importantly, Isaiah also has been called the miniature Bible because his book corresponds to the rest of the Bible books. For example, the first thirty-nine chapters of Isaiah remind us of the thirty-nine books of the Old Testament, and the twenty-seven remaining chapters take our mind to the message of grace and redemption found in the twenty-seven New Testament books. The prophet is called the prince of Old Testament prophets.

The Book

Penman: The four kings mentioned in the introduction reigned during this period (Isaiah 1:1), and Isaiah confirmed he was given the vision of this book. Several Jewish scholars believe that Isaiah penned thirty-nine books only; they claim that chapters 40–66 were written by someone else. The majority say the prophet foretold those events. But from all indications, Isaiah is the author of the book.

Person (s) addressed: The Jewish Nation

Period covered: Between 740–695 BC

Position of the book in the Bible: Twenty-third book

Purpose of the book: There are two basic aims of Isaiah's prophecy: Isaiah was to warn Judah that, if the people refused to repent, judgment was about to come upon them as God had already begun punishing the northern kingdom for their sins by using their worst enemy. Also, he was to prophecy concerning the coming of Jewish Messiah. In other words, even though God would punish them for their wrongdoings, at the same time he would also comfort them as they turned to him. That is the God of justice, love, and mercy.

Popular people in the book: Isaiah, Hezekiah, Uzziah

Places in the book: Judah, Israel

Particular events in the book: sin removes soundness and brings wounds (Isaiah 1:2–24), promise for Jerusalem (Isaiah 1:25–31), God's hatred for sin of pride (Isaiah 3:16–26), Ephraim joined with foe to fight Jerusalem (Isaiah 7:1–9), the Lord's sign (Isaiah 7:10–25), cursed people (Isaiah 5:8–25), Uzziah's death and the prophet's cleansing (Isaiah 6:1–8), Isaiah's wife and son (Isaiah 8:1–4), The king child was born (Isaiah 9:6), King Sennacherib's shameful defeat and disgraceful death (Isaiah chapter 37), King Hezekiah's restoration (Isaiah chapter 38), Babylonians humiliation (Isaiah chapters 46–47), Zion was comforted (Isaiah chapters 61–64), suffering servant (Isaiah chapters 52–53).

Person of Christ in the book: Prince of Peace (Isaiah 9:6)

Portrait of the book: Prophecy

The Contents

I. **The predictive statement of the prophet** (Isaiah 1–35)

(a) His common concern and convictions (Isaiah 1:1–5:30)

(b) His call, concept and compass (Isaiah 6:1–24:23)

(c) His chorus, cries and commands (Isaiah 25:1–35:10)

II. **The practical statesmanship of the prophet** (Isaiah 36–39)

(a) King's salvation (Isaiah 36:1–37:38)

(b) King's sickness (Isaiah 38:1–22)

(c) King's sin (Isaiah 39:1–8)

III. **The prophetic stature of the prophet** (Isaiah 40–66)

(a) Message of memorable comfort (Isaiah 40:1–48:22)

(b) Message of Messiah's coming (Isaiah 49:1–57:21)

(c) Message of millennium contents (Isaiah 58:1–66:24)

The Statistics

There are sixty-six chapters in Isaiah, 1, 292 verses, and 37, 044 words.

Conclusion

God's patience cannot stop him from punishing sinners and evil doers. As a compassionate father, he shows mercy to the one who turns to him for forgiveness. This is valuable. And the volume of letters of the prophet is for everyone.

Jeremiah

Introduction

Jeremiah means "Jehovah establishes". His father, Hilkiah, was a priest from Anathoth, a town about three miles from Jerusalem, the residents of which belonged to Benjamin's tribe. He was called into the prophetic office when his nation was to come to an end. It was a stormy era. The Babylonian armies were at the door. Able-bodied people were being deported into a strange land. The Temple where Jehovah was worshipped was soon to be destroyed. The young prophet at the time pleaded with persuasion that the people should listen to his warnings and cease from wickedness. Instead, Jeremiah, in return, received persecution and punishment from his own people. Of course, he encouraged Judah to surrender to the invaders. For fifty years, he preached and prophesied. He wept each time he thought about the humiliation his people would go through. This's why Jeremiah is known as the weeping prophet.

Meanwhile, before Judah stopped being a nation, some group of individuals forced the prophet to the Egyptians, and when Babylonians came and destroyed Jerusalem, the prophet's life was spared. His predictions were all fulfilled, and the book ends with Judah in the hand of Babylon (in modern-day Iraq).

The Book

Penman: Jeremiah

Person (s) addressed: Jewish People of Judah

Period covered: Approximately 625–585 BC

Position of the book in the Bible: Twenty-fourth book

Purpose of the book: Jeremiah intends to challenge leaders—kings and rulers in Judah—for supporting their subjects in their wrongdoings against God. He sternly condemned the people for following other gods. He felt they must be banished unless they changed. The prophet advised the nation to give up to the Babylonians, for the judgment came from God.

Popular people in the book: Jeremiah; Baruch, his secretary; Jehoiakim, the king who burned Jeremiah's first prophecy; Zedekiah, the last king of Judah

Places in the book: Judah, Egypt, Babylon

Particular events in the book: prophet purchased a field (Jeremiah 32:1–44), the Rechabites (Jeremiah 35:1–19).

Person of Christ in the book: The Potter (Jeremiah 18:6)

Portrait of the book: History, biography, and prophecy

The Contents

I. **The mandate of Jeremiah** (Jeremiah 1)

(a) God's call of the preacher (Jeremiah 1:1–10)

(b) God's complain of the people (Jeremiah 1:11–16)

(c) God's courageous protective power (Jeremiah 1:17–19)

II. **The message of Jeremiah** (Jeremiah 2–51)

(a) Judah's unfaithfulness noticed (Jeremiah 2:1–45:5)

(b) Judgment upon nations (Jeremiah 46:1–51:53)

(c) Justice utterly nearer (Jeremiah 51:54–64)

III. **The misery of Jeremiah** (Jeremiah 52)

(a) Shameful death of the king (Jeremiah 52:1–11)

(b) Sudden destruction of the city (Jeremiah 52:12–30)

(c) Sound demeanour of the monarch (Jeremiah 52:31–34)

The Statistics

There are fifty-two chapters in Jeremiah, 1, 364 verses, and 42, 654 words.

Conclusion

The prophecy of Jeremiah was timeless, and it stands as a caution for all eras with regard to the law of reaping. What you sow is what you reap. Judah sinned and was punished. No one escapes God's divine judgment. The only way out is through repentance, obedience, and trusting the only wise God. Everyone gets what he or she deserves. The shortcut to all these is to fear and honour God with our lives. A further reason we should be loyal and submissive to God's control is that the Bible asks, "Can the Ethiopian change his skin, or the leopard his spots? Then may ye also do good, that are accustomed to do evil (Jeremiah 13:23)." Since the answer is no, then I challenge you to surrender to the Potter, for we are absolutely nothing but clay in his hand.

Lamentations

Introduction

Lamentations is a collection of five songs written by Jeremiah, who witnessed the most tragic event that ever occurred in Jewish nation's history. The prophet expressed great grief and anguish over the wrath that God poured out on his own chosen people. Though Jeremiah never blamed God for any wrongdoing, he cried, wept, groaned, and mourned. The book of Lamentations is borne out of the prophet's experiences of his people's tragedy because of their refusal to adhere to warnings. This resulted in an outpouring of sadness over the destruction of Jerusalem by the Babylonian king.

The Book

Penman: The unnamed writer of the book was a witness to the tragic events that took place in the Jewish land. Jewish tradition and some other evidence agree that prophet Jeremiah was the penman (2 Chronicles 35:25).

Person (s) addressed: Jewish People of the south

Period covered: About 585 BC

Position of the book in the Bible: Twenty-fifth book

Purpose of the book: The book aims to show how sad and sorry the people were in Babylon and to indicate that they had caused their problem, not God. Above all, the book was meant to show that God's mercy endures forever. It also showed his willingness to bring the people back into their homeland when they were ready.

Popular people in the book: Jeremiah

Places in the book: Jerusalem, Babylon, Edom, Uz

Particular events in the book: helplessness due to sin (Lamentations 1:1–17), God's anger, forgotten sabbath and enemy's mockery (Lamentations 2:1–22), bear the yoke in your youth (Lamentations 3:27).

Person of Christ in the book: The Man of Sorrow (Lamentations 2:11)

Portrait of the book: History, biography and prophecy

The Contents

I. Wretchedness of the people of Jerusalem (Lamentations 1 and 5)

(a) The cry (Lamentations 1:1–17)

amentations 1:18–22)

(c) The contrition (Lamentations 5:1–22)

II. **Wrath against the people of Jehovah** (Lamentations 2 and 4)

(a) Retribution and repentance confirmed (Lamentations 2:1–22)

(b) Past and present of Judah contrasted (Lamentations 4:1–20)

(c) Edom and Judah rewards compared (Lamentations 4: 21–22)

III. **Woe of the prophet Jeremiah** (Lamentations 3)

(a) A Spiritual renewal (Lamentations 3:1–42)

(b) A sorrowful recording (Lamentations 3:43–51)

(c) A supplication for restoration (Lamentations 3:52–66)

The Statistics

There are five chapters in Lamentations, 154 verses, and 3, 415 words.

Conclusion

God in his creative, awesome power, at any time, can use anything to achieve his purpose without bias. He chastised his own peculiar people through their enemy, the Babylonians. The fall of Jerusalem, enslavement of the people, and their torture and starvation did not mean they had been forgotten or written off as many assume today. God, at the same moment, immediately stretched his loving hands towards them to receive them back. We are aware that God cures backsliders and restores them to fellowship. He heals diseases and binds wounds. He hates sin but loves sinners. God also can save and give people life only if they can call on him in genuine repentance.

Ezekiel

Introduction

Comprehensive biographical information concerning this seer is not common, but the period and place of the servant of God are well known. Basically, Ezekiel descended from a priestly ancestry, and his prophetic interests may be envisaged from the start of this book through the end of it (Wevers 1976, 23).

A young priest of Jerusalem, Ezekiel was among captives taken to Babylon by Nebuchadnezzar during his second invasion. While in exile, about five years after his capture, Ezekiel was called into a prophetic ministry. *Ezekiel* means "strengthened by God". He ministered to his fellow deportees and spoke of coming divine judgment for the rest of the people in Jerusalem. His message was not accepted by other Jews in Babylon. After his prophecies came to pass, people desired to hear the prophet. Having shown interest to the warnings, Ezekiel revealed the future hope and comforted them. The prophet's work lasted over twenty-three years, and tradition has it that he was killed by his fellow captives because he opposed their idol worship.

The Book

Penman: According to Ezekiel 1:1–3, the young priest must have penned it.

Person (s) addressed: Those captives in Babylon

Period covered: Between 590–570 BC

Position of the book in the Bible: Twenty-sixth book

Purpose of the book: The aim of the book was to let the captives in Babylon know that, after they have accepted prophet's message, God would take them back to their land and would certainly punish remaining people in Judah who were living without God.

Popular people in the book: Ezekiel, the people of Judah who were still in their country, and those in Babylon

Places in the book: Judea, Babylon, River Chebar, Telabib

Particular events in the book: idolatry in the Temple (Ezekiel 8:1–18), idolaters killed (Ezekiel 9:1–11), unlawful wife (Ezekiel 16:1–63), two eagles story (Ezekiel 17:1–24), sign of the death of the young prophet's wife (Ezekiel 24:15–27), a valley filled with dry bones (Ezekiel 37:1–28), the healing river (Ezekiel 47:1–23).

Person of Christ in the book: Holy One in Israel (Ezekiel 39:7)

Portrait of the book: History and prophecy

The Contents

I. **Predictions about Judah before its fall** (Ezekiel 1–24)

(a) Calls and commissions (Ezekiel 1:1–3:27)

(b) Commands and condemns (Ezekiel 4:1–20, 27–32)

(c) Compensates and commemorates (Ezekiel 20:33–24:27)

II. **Predictions about Judah in the midst of its foes** (Ezekiel 25–32)

(a) Prophecy concerning Ammon and Moab (Ezekiel 25:1–11)

(b) Prophecy concerning Edom and Philistia (Ezekiel 25:12–17)

(c) Prophecy concerning Tyre, Sidon, and Egypt (Ezekiel 26:1–32:32)

III. **Predictions about Judah and its future** (Ezekiel 33–48)

(a) People's troubles removed (Ezekiel 33:1–36:38)

(b) People's tribes regrouped and Temple reconstructed (Ezekiel 37:1–47:23)

(c) People's title restored (Ezekiel 48:1–35)

The Statistics

There are forty-eight chapters in Ezekiel, 1, 273 verses, and 39, 407 words.

Conclusion

Ezekiel is called the book of vision. This author was a dedicated trained priest of Judah who later, while in Babylon, became a prophet. Buzi, the priest, was Ezekiel's father. After Judah's captivity, the people were restored as promised and never again driven away from their God-given family home. So, Ezekiel faithfully ministered to the people despite all the problems he encountered; he represented God as his spokesman. You can become another Ezekiel in your generation.

Daniel

Introduction

Daniel was about 17 years old when he was taken to Babylon by king Nebuchadnezzar in 605 BC along with other Hebrew able-bodied young men. Irrespective of his situation as captive, Daniel received an education in the king's courts so he could serve as an administrator in the kingdom that later rose to a high position. He was promoted from one level to another. Daniel's trust, faithfulness, and uncompromising stand provided an avenue through which his God could demonstrate his great power among the heathen.

For this reason, when Persia took over from Babylon in 538 BC, the same Daniel served the next new government. He and his three friends were subjected to extreme persecution, and they survived only by the intervention of God. He lived nearly all his long life there. His prophecies and visions were concerned largely with the four great empires, and his dreams pointed to the end of human rule in the entire universe. However, he remained a loyal witness and trusted servant of God in such a godless society. Daniel was faithful to the end.

The Book

Penman: Some scholars have various opinions regarding the authorship of Daniel, especially Porphyry in the third century, who said Daniel was a fictitious character, not real person. Later, in the seventeenth and eighteenth centuries, many Jews and church fathers strongly attested that the penman must be Daniel the prophet because Jesus and Ezekiel both mentioned Daniel as the author. The Bible itself confirms that he wrote the book (Mathew 24:15; Ezekiel 14:14, 20; 28:3; Daniel 7:2; 8:1; 9:2; 12:4).

Person (s) addressed: Daniel's fellow captives (Hebrews) in Babylon

Period covered: Book of Daniel was written in sixth century about 536 BC

Position of the book in the Bible: Twenty-seventh book

Purpose of the book: It is to encourage the Jewish individuals who are in a foreign land—even Babylon—that God is still in control and that, no matter what had transpired between God and Israel, Israel would remain God's favourite. In God's future endeavours, the people would work side by side with him. In other words, God's remembrance of his people would lead to their restoration.

Popular people in the book: Nebuchadnezzar, Belshazzar, Darius, Daniel, three Hebrew boys

Places in the book: Judah, Babylon

Particular events in the book: decision that determines destiny (Daniel 1:8), interpretation of the king's dream and Daniel's reward (Daniel 2:1–49), an image of gold (Daniel 3:1–30), Nebuchadnezzar repents (Daniel4:1–37), Belshazzar's death (Daniel 5:1–37), Darius, Daniel, and the den of lions (Daniel 6:1–28), dream of four beasts (Daniel 7:1–28), ram and goat nations

(Daniel 8:1–27), Daniel's sorrow and prayer (Daniel 9:1–27), Daniel's vision of a man and the man speaks (Daniel 10:2–21).

Person of Christ in the book: The Fourth Man (Daniel 3:25)

Portrait of the book: Prophecy

The Contents

I. **Daniel and his Hebrew friends** (Daniel 1–6)

(a) Hours of trials and temptations (Daniel 1:1–3:30)

(b) Hours of testimony and truthfulness (Daniel 4:1–5:31)

(c) Hours of temerity and triumph (Daniel 6:1–28)

II. **Daniel and his hilarious facts** (Daniel 7–11)

(a) Dream of beasts (Daniel 7:1–28)

(b) Dreads of brokenness (Daniel 8:1–27)

(c) Darius the beloved (Daniel 9:1–11:45)

III. **Daniel and his heralding future** (Daniel 12)

(a) The tribulation elucidated (Daniel 12:1–4)

(b) The truth is emphasized (Daniel 12:5–9)

(c) The times ensured (Daniel 12:10–13)

The Statistics

There are twelve chapters in Daniel, 357 verses, and 11, 606 words.

Conclusion

Daniel means "God is the judge". His faithfulness was outstanding. Daniel lived in Babylon without supervision, yet he maintained and portrayed godliness in such a crucial and heathen society. Prophet Daniel became God's representative in the midst of his colleagues in government. The prophet and his chums were highly rewarded. Are your services to God today mixed up with hypocrisy and compromise? God is our judge indeed. God watches and will reward us.

Hosea

Introduction

The book of Hosea is the longest book of the twelve minor prophets' writings. Prophet Hosea was the last messenger sent by God to his people in Israel, in the northern kingdom, prior to its destruction by the Assyrians. In his book, Hosea called the kingdom by various names such as Israel, Ephraim, and Samaria.

The prophet proved information regarding his wife who turned into a prostitute. He saw that Israel had also behaved like a prostitute by following other gods. Hosea had married Gomer and had three children. Gomer, the wife of the prophet, was going after other men. In fact, she left Hosea's home and went into prostitution. But Prophet Hosea sought her and brought her back to his house to continue living with him. She then fathered Jezreel, Lo–ruhamah, and Lo–ammi.

Hosea means "salvation". Its Greek form is *Jesus*. *Gomer* means "heat". This is the name of two persons in the Bible: the eldest son of Japheth, and Hosea's unfaithful wife. *Jezreel*, the name of their first son, means "God sows". *Lo–ammi*, the name of the second son, means "not my people". And *Lo–ruhamah*, the name of the third son, means "not favoured" or "no pity". Anyway, Hosea did obey God's command.

The Book

Penman: Hosea penned the book

Person (s) addressed: Northern Israel

Period covered: Since Hosea took over as a prophet immediately after Prophet Amos, the suitable subjection of the writing of his book would be around 724 BC.

Position of the book in the Bible: Twenty-eighth book

Purpose of the book: The book's aim is to caution the people of Israel concerning their unfaithfulness to God. This is because the book reveals to us that Hosea represents God. Gomer, his wife, depicts Israel. So, Israel was unfaithful to God as Gomer was to him. She played harlotry by worshipping idols instead of God, the legal husband.

Popular people in the book: Hosea, Gomer

Places in the book: Samaria, Valley of Jezreel

Particular events in the book: Hosea's marriage (Hosea 1:1–9), Ephraim rebuked, and Israel served for a wife (Hosea 12:1–14), God's plea and promise for the people (Hosea 14:1–9).

Person of Christ in the book: The Forsaken Husband (Hosea chapter 4:1–19)

Portrait of the book: Prophecy

The Contents

I. A heartbroken prophet (Hosea 1–3)

(a) Signs of his children (Hosea 1:1–11)

(b) Sin of his wife (Hosea 2:1–23)

(c) Salvation for his life (Hosea 3:1–5)

II. A people burdened with hard times (Hosea 4–13)

(a) The people are polluted (Hosea 4:1–7:16)

(b) The people are punished (Hosea 8:1–10:17)

(c) The people are pardoned (Hosea 11:1–13:16)

III. A healing bestowed praise (Hosea 14)

(a) Fatherless heard (Hosea 14:1–3)

(b) Fruitlessness healed (Hosea 14:4–8)

(c) Faithfulness hailed (Hosea 14:9)

The Statistics

There are fourteen chapters in Hosea, 197 verses, and 5, 175 words.

Conclusion

We have come to the end of the book of Hosea. Let us not easily forget that the main part of the prophet's message focused on his family life. Israel, the northern kingdom, had forsaken her husband and had gone after heathen gods and has prostituted itself. That was an unfaithful act! According to the following passages those who practice them are prostitutes, just as Gomer (Hosea 4:1–2; 10–14, 16; 5:5; 6:8–10). Sins such as unfaithfulness, swearing, deception, murder, stealing of any type, adultery, rebellion, idolatry, disobedience, and pride must be avoided. Remember, God's love for us is powerful and has no end. Who else could have paid the price to redeem us from the slavery of our wrong choices? Who loves and has not given up on us and delights our love in return? No one else but the Lord God, King of Glory. His gift to us is but love; our gift to Him should be to surrender our will and ambitions to him.

Joel

Introduction

Imagine a prophecy of God's humble servant, Moses, which he made many years ago in his last writing. Then address Israel in Deuteronomy chapter twenty-eight and see it fulfilled. He warned the people to obey the commandment of God. If they disobeyed, locusts would surely pay a sudden destructive visit that would result in total loss of their vegetation, which would bring about famine.

In his book, Joel, the son of Pethuel, described the desolation of Judah by a swarm of locusts. He built on past events and looked ahead into the future, meaning that what locusts and drought had done before was exactly what an army from the north would later do. Joel finally described the battle that would bring about the restoration of Israel and the establishment of the millennium kingdom.

Joel predicted the outpouring of the Spirit of God on all flesh and the wonders that would follow. Apostle Peter quotes him on the day of Pentecost. Read Joel chapter 2:28–32 and Acts 2. No wonder he is known as "the prophet of Pentecost" and he has been called the John the Baptist of the Old Testament. *Joel* means "Jehovah is God".

The Book

Penman: Nothing much is known of this prophet. We don't know where he lived. We don't know any further information about his family life except that his father was Pethuel. Joel may not have been a priest since he particularly addressed them in Joel 2:15–17.

Person (s) addressed: Judah, the southern kingdom

Period covered: Certainly, the date of writing of this book is unknown. Yet the fact remains that Joel did not record any king, possibly because it was written when Jehoiada, the high priest, was ruling on behalf of Joash, who was just a little lad during the time, and that was between 830–791 BC.

Position of the book in the Bible: Twenty-ninth book

Purpose of the book: The purpose of Joel's writing was to warn the people of Judah to turn to God quickly as he would not delay judging them for their sin of idolatry. It was also to inform all people about the Day of the Lord, which will surely come and will close the entire history of man. It was a call for the change of life.

Popular people in the book: Joel, Jewish people

Places in the book: Zion, Valley of Jehoshaphat

Particular events in the book: A call to repentance (Joel 22:1–32).

Person of Christ in the book: The Judge (Joel 3:12)

Portrait of the book: Prophecy

The Contents

I. **Declaration of the plague and famine** (Joel 1)

(a) Persons and problems (Joel 1:1–7)

(b) Priests and products (Joel 1:8–10, 11–12, 13–16, 17–18)

(c) Prophet and plea (Joel 1:19–20)

II. **Description of the perdition and foes** (Joel 2:1–11)

(a) The land (Joel 2:1)

(b) The locusts (Joel 2:2–10)

(c) The Lord (Joel 2:11)

III. **Divine promise and the forgiveness** (Joel 2:12–3:21)

(a) Call to return (Joel 2:12–14)

(b) Complete repentance (Joel 2:15–17)

(c) Committed redeemed (Joel 2:18–3:21)

The Statistics

There are three chapters in Joel, 73 verses, and 2, 034 words.

Conclusion

Sin truly hurts. Calamity came upon Judah following the nation's departure from God. Prophet Joel urged individuals in the land to seek the face of the Lord so that judgment of an army of locusts from the north would not come to devour the inhabitants, but those who repented would be delivered and shown mercy. Let us learn from Joel's people and serve the Lord.

Amos

Introduction

Amos was sent to the northern Israel as a prophet at the time the land witnessed prosperity and moral laxity. It might interest you to know that this country man, Amos, a former successful farmer from the southern kingdom, was not trained in one of the schools of the prophets. His name means "burden bearer", and he declared judgment against surrounding nations. He spoke out vehemently for justice against the religious leaders and rich men of his day, for which he was driven away from the royal sanctuary at Bethel.

We read of visions that support his stern message to the people and yet there was unwillingness to change. As always, if the people would have listened and repented, goodness and mercy would have followed. But if they ignored this advice, they would have to dance to the tune of the bitter music of impending judgment for their injustice.

Prophet Amos saw a vision of God roaring as a lion from Mount Zion in his holy Temple, saying that he would examine the people with a "plumb line" and would cause them to scatter all over the universe. Amos did see that these individuals would eventually, at last, be restored.

The Book

Penman: Amos probably wrote this book at the end of the rule of Jeroboam II, who reigned in Israel between 793–753 BC.

Person (s) addressed: Northern kingdom of Israel

Period covered: Approximately 760 BC

Position of the book in the Bible: Thirtieth book

Purpose of the book: During this time, Bethel was still one of the cities in the north where golden calves were being worshipped. So, Amos warned Israel to come back to God and begin to live righteous lives; otherwise, the people would have to face God's anger.

Popular people in the book: Amos, Amaziah, Jeroboam

Places in the book: Northern kingdom of Israel, Samaria, Bethel, Judah

Particular events in the book: Amaziah the priest's attack on the prophet and Amos' reply (Amos 7:1–17).

Person of Christ in the book: Plumb Line (Amos 7:9)

Portrait of the book: Prophecy

The Contents

I. **Vigilance of Amos, the prophet** (Amos 1–2)

(a) Judgment on Damascus, Gaza, and Tyre (Amos 1:1–10)

(b) Judgment on Edom, Moab, and Ammon (Amos 1:11–2:3)

(c) Judgment on Judah and Israel only (Amos 2:4–16)

II. **Voice of Amos, the prophet** (Amos 3–6)

(a) Israel's privileges despised (Amos 3:1–15)

(b) Israel's perversity described (Amos 4:1–13)

(c) Israel's punishment determined (Amos 5:1–6:14)

III. **Visions of Amos, the prophet** (Amos 7–9)

(a) The fire (Amos 7:1–17)

(b) The fruit (Amos 8:1–14)

(c) The future (Amos 9:1–15)

The Statistics

There are nine chapters in Amos, 146 verses, and 4, 217 words.

Conclusion

Anyone who holds the belief that only those called into the ministry with a good educational background are better materials for the work, especially individuals with Bible training experience, may be making a mistake. Amos was just an ordinary husbandman when God needed him to go to Bethel and warned Jeroboam, Amaziah, and those rich men in the land who exploited the poor. He also cautioned spiritual officials who sold themselves unto unrighteousness to repent of their wickedness and turn from their evil ways.

If you are sincerely called of God, be aware that education shall not and will never be an obstacle. Notwithstanding, education plus anointing when called by God leads to breakthroughs. Education in itself is excellent. Amos the prophet was an example of that. Dedication and commitment play essential roles in the ministry.

Obadiah

Introduction

Obadiah means "servant of Jehovah." Nothing much is known of this prophet. His book is the shortest book in the Hebrew Bible and the third shortest in the entire Bible. About twelve men bear his name. Prophet Obadiah was called to preach against Edom (the present Jordan). There was long-time enmity between the twin brothers, Esau and Jacob. Esau's descendants were the Edomites, and Jacob's were the Israelites.

When the king of Babylon invaded the city of Jerusalem, the people of Edom were so excited to hear that tragedy had fallen upon their brothers. Also, the Edomites captured Jewish refugees who wanted to escape the siege and handed them over to the formidable army of Babylon. For this single action of Edom, God told Obadiah to speak about Edom's destruction (Obadiah 1:15). The way we treat other people, whether in public or private, is the way we can expect the Lord to treat us. That is the central message of this book.

The Book

Penman: Prophet Obadiah.

Person (s) addressed: The Edomites

Period covered: 843 BC

Position of the book in the Bible: Thirty-first book

Purpose of the book: It is to inform Israel's brother, Edom, that God will punish him for supporting his brother's enemy and his part in stolen their goods in Jerusalem.

Popular people in the book: Obadiah, Edom, Esau

Places in the book: Edom, Judah

Particular events in the book: The vision of Obadiah (Obadiah 1:1).

Person of Christ in the book: Mount Zion (Obadiah verse 21)

Portrait of the book: Prophecy

The Contents

I. **The rejection of Edom announced** (Obadiah 1:1–9)

(a) Edom's overthrown declared (Obadiah 1:1–2)

(b) Edom's overthrown described (Obadiah 1:3–7)

(c) Edom's overthrown deserved (Obadiah 1:8–9)

II. **The reasons for the enemy's animadvert** (Obadiah 1:10–16)

(a) Edom encouraged the foes of their brutality (Obadiah 1:10–11)

(b) Edom enjoyed the fall of his own brethren (Obadiah 1:12–13)

(c) Edom enslaved fugitives without backup (Obadiah 1:14–16)

III. **The restoration ensured contra antichrist** (Obadiah 1:17–21)

(a) The character of Israel's deliverance (Obadiah 1:17a)

(b) The completeness of Israel's deliverance (Obadiah 1:17b–20)

(c) The conclusion of Israel's deliverance (Obadiah 1:21)

The Statistics

There is only one chapter in Obadiah, 21 verses, and 670 words.

Conclusion

Obadiah spoke against Edom, the other nations, and the people of Israel. Edom was not offered options and had to be destroyed. Edom did not show mercy or hear the pleas of God's children. As a result, God did not spare it. The way we treat God's servants counts heavily. They should be treated with respect and not worshipped. Rather, they must be honoured because the Bible supports that. God had numbered their hairs (Matthew 10:30). What a privilege to be a child of God!

Jonah

Introduction

Jonah in Hebrew means "dove". Prophet Jonah's book contains personal life experience information. He ministered in Israel during the rule of King Jeroboam II. He was sent by God to the people of Nineveh, Assyria's capital. Jonah was to approach them with God's Word; if they fail to repent of their wickedness, they would face his divine judgment. This cruel nation flayed their enemies alive, made heaps of their skulls, and did other dreadful deeds. Besides, Nineveh was the most formidable city ever known at the time, with one-hundred-foot-high walls and towers that ascended one hundred feet higher. Its walls were so thick that three chariots could drive on top of them side by side. Moreover, the city was enveloped by a moat that was almost 150 feet across and sixty feet deep. This is where Jonah was sent to warn the people. Instead, he fled to Tarshish (present-day Spain) and finally saw himself in the belly of a big fish. When he was vomited onto dry land after three days, he decided to obey God's command. He went to Nineveh, but the prophet was greatly unhappy and dissatisfied; hence, God would no longer destroy them.

Nevertheless, Jonah's journal is a very useful book of the Bible. It pictures the death, burial, and resurrection of Christ. Jesus clearly and intently quoted Jonah in Matthew's Gospel (12:40–41; 16:4).

The Book

Penman: Jonah penned the book (Jonah 1:1)

Person (s) addressed: Israel, the northern kingdom

Period covered: King Jeroboam, who reigned from about 791–751 BC, was still on the throne during the era in which Jonah ministered. It is then assumed the date of this book should be around 775 BC.

Position of the book in the Bible: Thirty-second book

Purpose of the book: The book's aim is to reveal that obedience to God's Word leads to life; that salvation is for everyone irrespective of race, nationality, colour, whether Jews or Gentiles; and that God honours those who honour him. Although God had established a covenant relationship with his people, the Jews, through Abraham, yet he did not reject the rest of mankind, especially anyone who seeks him.

Popular people in the book: Jonah, Jeroboam II

Places in the book: Israel, Nineveh

Particular events in the book: Jonah pushed into the sea, was swallowed up by a fish, and slept in its belly for three days (Jonah 1:1–17), the prophet's prayer while in whale's belly (Jonah 2:1–10),

the city's repentance and God's change of heart (Jonah 3:1–10), Jonah's displeasure and gourd's disappearance (Jonah 4:1–11).

Person of Christ in the book: The Merciful One (Jonah 3:10)

Portrait of the book: History and prophecy

The Contents

I. Jonah's disobedience and deliverance (Jonah 1–2)

(a) His profile (Jonah 1:1–3)

(b) His problem (Jonah 1:4–17)

(c) His prayer (Jonah 2:1–10)

II. Jonah's declaration and discovery (Jonah 3)

(a) Jonah's message (Jonah 3:1–4)

(b) Nineveh's memorandum (Jonah 3:5–9)

(c) God's mercy (Jonah 3:10)

III. Jonah's displeasure and distress (Jonah 4)

(a) Unjustified anger (Jonah 4:1–3)

(b) Unconcerned attitude (Jonah 4:4–9)

(c) Unquestionable (alpha and omega) author (Jonah 4:10–11)

The Statistics

There are four chapters in Jonah, 48 verses, and 1, 321 words.

Conclusion

Christians have been commissioned to take the Good News of salvation to the dying world as in Nineveh of old! There may be individuals who are indifferent to us and our faith; still, every effort should be made to reach them for the sake of their souls. At the first attempt, this might look impossible and discouraging, but if we persist and obey the Lord, then we shall see the unsaved turning to God. will result walking death living again. When Jonah later obeyed, the people of Nineveh surrendered to God, even though Jonah misunderstood God as most of us do. God demonstrated in the book of Jonah that he is God of mercy, love, and compassion. He also respects anyone who exercises faith in him.

Micah

Introduction

Micah means "who is like Jehovah". He was from Moresheth-Gath, a town close to the Philistine border about twenty-four miles southwest of the city of Jerusalem. He was serving as a prophet at the same time Prophet Isaiah was serving, but he was not from a high social class. During the same period, Hosea ministered to the north of Israel. Micah spoke strongly not only against Jerusalem, but to Samaria denouncing people, prophets, priests, and princes alike for their iniquities that made retribution unavoidable. He thoughtfully addressed the matter of oppression of the mendicant by affluent individuals.

In 5:2, Micah predicted that the Messiah would be born in Bethlehem Ephrathah. He was very specific here because there is another Bethlehem up north. When Jesus came, he quoted the book of Micah in Matthew 2:6, showing the book's significance.

The Book

Penman: The work was attributed to Prophet Micah. He is the only prophet whose words are attributed to him in another prophet book (Jeremiah 26:18).

Person (s) addressed: Southern and northern kingdoms (Judah and Israel)

Period covered: Prophet Micah lived during the rules of Jotham, Ahaz, and Hezekiah, about 735–683 BC.

Position of the book in the Bible: Thirty-third book

Purpose of the book: The primary aim of Micah is to demonstrate the concern of the Lord God for justice. It focuses on calling the people back to practical righteousness in both south and north.

Popular people in the book: Micah, leaders in Judah

Places in the book: Jerusalem, Samaria, Bethlehem

Particular events in the book: Idol destroyed (Micah 5:8–15)

Person of Christ in the book: The Ruler (Micah 5:2)

Portrait of the book: Prophetical

The Contents

I. **A prediction of retribution** (Micah 1–3)

(a) Transgressions of people and punishment (Micah 1:16–2:13)

(b) Transgressions of princes and prophets (Micah 3:1–10)

(c) Transgressions of priests and peril (Micah 3:11–12)

II. **A promise of restoration** (Micah 4–6)

(a) The millennial reign (Micah 4:1–13)

(b) The Messiah's rule (Micah 5:1–15)

(c) The message of ruin (Micah 6:1–16)

III. **A plea to return** (Micah 7)

(a) The nation's sorrow (Micah 7:1–6)

(b) The nation's source (Micah 7:7)

(c) The nation's saviour (Micah 7:8–20)

The Statistics

There are seven chapters in Micah,105 verses, and 3, 153 words.

Conclusion

Micah was not afraid to speak to the rich of his day who used their position to torture the helpless poor. He told the people to cease from wickedness. The false prophets who would not do God's work without profit were rebuked, the priests who neglected their jobs did not find it easy with him, and even the princes of the land were scolded. Idolatry and all manner of evil practices brought about the downfall of a blissful nation. Prophet Micah did not spare anyone. Never take kickbacks (bribes) to create and increase injustice within the vicinity of your jurisdiction as many so-called ministers of God do today. Protect the environment where you are. Make it a corrupt-free place or area. Watch and mark those who do that. Micah defended the poor. From the book we find that God is still interested in the poor. He will not allow the wicked rich go unpunished. The Lord God frowns at those who disobey him; he desires everyone to live a humble life.

Nahum

Introduction

Nahum means "comforter". The book of Nahum supplements the prophecy of Jonah, who recorded that the people of Nineveh repented of their evil ways after Jonah warned them of the coming doom. While in Nahum, they returned and sold themselves in iniquity. Now they turned to their old lives and invited the wrath of God outright.

The Elkoshite then centres his message on the brutal attitude of the Assyrian military men who were absolutely inhumane. They had just taken the northern kingdom into slavery. It should be noted that the Assyrians were once used as instruments in the hand of God against his people. However, Prophet Nahum comforted God's people, assuring them that their task masters and war-like enemy would soon be smitten by God for their evil ways and ill treatment against Israel.

The Book

Penman: Nothing much is known concerning this prophet, only that his hometown was Elkosh. The designation Elkoshite, as seen in Nahum 1:1 has given rise to much speculation as to the prophet's origin. Some scholars believe that Elkosh was a village in Assyria. Others agree it was a town southwest of Jerusalem. Yet others hold that Capernaum in Galilee was his birthplace. The fact that the penman identifies himself as Nahum the Elkoshite suggests that he is likely to be the book's author.

Person (s) addressed: The Ninevites

Period covered: Probably written in the half century after Assyria army defeated No–Amon (Thebes), the Egyptian capital, in 663 BC. Nahum states this in his book. It must have been penned before Babylonians destroyed Nineveh in 612 BC. The book of Nahum was likely written between these events.

Position of the book in the Bible: Thirty-fourth book

Purpose of the book: The book intends to reveal exactly what happened to Nineveh, which God did not destroy earlier when Jonah preached to them. The prophet wanted to assure God's people that Nineveh, the Assyrian's capital city, must surely be judged.

Popular people in the book: Nahum, people of Nineveh

Places in the Book: Nineveh, Thebes, Ethiopia, Egypt, Libya

Particular events in the book: The Lord's judgment on Nineveh (Nahum 3:3).

Person of Christ in the book: The Avenger (Nahum 1:2, 15)

Portrait of the book: Prophecy

The Contents

I. **Declaration of the destruction of Nineveh** (Nahum 1)

(a) God's patience and his passion (Nahum 1:1–3a)

(b) God's power and his pre–eminence (Nahum 1:3b–8)

(c) God's purpose and his protection (Nahum 1:9–15)

II. **Description of the destruction of Nineveh** (Nahum 2)

(a) The signal of its condemnation (Nahum 2:1–3)

(b) The siege of its capital (Nahum 2:4–12)

(c) The sack of its chariots cocksure (Nahum 2:13)

III. **Deserved destruction of Nineveh** (Nahum 3)

(a) The filthiness of the city (Nahum 3:1–7)

(b) The fear of the city (Nahum 3:8–13)

(c) The fall of the city (Nahum 3:14–19)

The Statistics

There are three chapters in Nahum, 47, verses and 1, 285 words.

Conclusion

God's people are so precious in his sight. No one who maltreats the children of God will ever go unpunished. Nineveh was forgiven when Jonah preached, but their improved behaviour did not last long. They went back to their sins without knowing that Jonah would not come to them the second time. So, what they finally received was doom instead of mercy.

However, Nahum pinpoints very loud and clear that God controls all nations of the world, that he must punish the enemies of those who trust in him, and that we should treat others as we would like them to treat us. We all must follow God's Word. It does not matter whether you're from Nineveh, Europe, Africa, Asia, or the States. The standard of the Word of God is the same. The solution is simple: obey God's Word.

Habakkuk

Introduction

Habakkuk means "embrace". He was called to be a prophet by God and was the last prophet who brought God's Word to the people of Judah before its fall. During this period, the people of Judah had gone deep into the worship of other gods and had followed customs and practices of their neighbouring countries. His own and the only remaining kingdom had totally forsaken him. Prophet Habakkuk saw injustice and ungodliness in the land. People had drifted away from God.

Habakkuk wondered why God kept silent even after seeing all the atrocities, and still refused to do something. Habakkuk has sometimes been called "the doubting Thomas of the OT." (MacDonald 1995, 1143). In response to Habakkuk's prayer, God revealed to him the nature of punishment by which he would correct the people with. The instrument would be the evil Babylon. Prophet Habakkuk again was displeased hearing this. Later the Lord of hosts plainly told him that, even though Babylon would be used, yet they would, in return, receive greater humiliation. His encounter with God turned him around; he saw a vision of God and of himself.

The Book

Penman: A Judean prophet choir whose family lineage and place of residence completely unknown had been assigned to this book (Habakkuk 1:1; 3:1, 19).

Person (s) addressed: Judah (southern kingdom)

Period covered: Scholars place Habakkuk during the rule of either of the following notable kings: Manasseh, the evil king; Josiah, the revivalist; or Jehoiakim. It was between 624–605 BC, about twenty-five years before the prophet's message came to pass.

Position of the book in the Bible: Thirty-fifth book

Purpose of the book: Habakkuk intended to inform the general public that wrongdoing will never go unnoticed or bypassed without receiving its proper justice. The doers shall not escape. It also contains conversations between God and his servant, the prophet, concerning Judah's rebellion and the Babylonians' wickedness.

Popular people in the book: Habakkuk, Chaldeans

Places in the book: Judah, Babylon

Particular events in the book: God's eyes (Habakkuk 1:12), write the vision (Habakkuk 2:1–4), woe to them (Habakkuk 2:5–20), Habakkuk complaint and prayer (Habakkuk 3:1–19).

Person of Christ in the book: Our Strength (Habakkuk chapter 3:19)

Portrait of the book: Prophecy

The Contents

I. **The troubled prophet** (Habakkuk 1)

(a) Indignation of the crimes (Habakkuk 1:1–4)

(b) Invincibility of the Chaldeans (Habakkuk 1:5–11)

(c) Iniquity of their cruelty (Habakkuk 1:12–17)

II. **The trained prophet** (Habakkuk 2)

(a) Write the vision clearly to be seen (Habakkuk 2:1–4)

(b) Watch the vast catalogues of sins (Habakkuk 2:5–19)

(c) Worship the veneration commended Still (Habakkuk 2:20)

III. **The triumphant prophet** (Habakkuk 3)

(a) His faith submits (Habakkuk 3:1–2)

(b) His faith satisfies (Habakkuk 3:3–16)

(c) His faith stimulates (Habakkuk 3:17–19)

The Statistics

There are three chapters in Habakkuk, 56 verses, and 1, 474 words.

Conclusion

The book of Habakkuk is the book of mysteries of providence. Any country, people, or individual who does not trust in God is destined to fail no matter their capabilities. At times the wicked seem to be doing well while the Christians are chastised. Obviously, the success of the wicked lasts only for a short time. One thing is sure—God will not forget those whose trust is in him. And as many as put their confidence in God shall never be ashamed because the just shall live by faith (Habakkuk 2:4).

Zephaniah

Introduction

Zephaniah means "Jehovah hides". This is the name of several people in the Hebrew Scripture. The prophet was the great grandson of Hezekiah, the good king of Judah. He ministered in the land at the time of Josiah, who reformed the entire nation and turned the people to God. He was motivated by Zephaniah's message. It was just a brief term of revival, and the city fell to Babylonian soldiers. The evil that Zephaniah spoke against in this writing were the evils of which his distant cousin, godly King Josiah, wept over.

The prophet was furious and agitated at this season, not only against Judah but at Judah's neighbouring countries and their people. He predicted God's judgment of them. He also stressed the point that God would deliver the good people and would reign over the entire universe from the city of Jerusalem. Meanwhile, Zephaniah had great royal connections.

The Book

Penman: Even though this man was of royal decent, that was not enough reason for him to avert challenging the religious and royal throne of his day. Zephaniah penned this book.

Person (s) addressed: Judah (The southern kingdom)

Period covered: Approximately between 625–611 BC

Position of the book in the Bible: Thirty-sixth book

Purpose of the book: Zephaniah revealed to Judah the coming day of the Lord's wrath on Judah and other nations, that which must surely happen. It showed them that sin must be judged. Those who honoured and respected his person would be saved.

Popular people in the book: Zephaniah, citizens of Judah

Places in the book: Jerusalem, the Fish Gate, Gaza, Ashkelon, Ashdod, Ekron, Moab, Ammon, Ethiopia, Assyria

Particular events in the book: judgment on Judah (Zephaniah 2:6), judgment on nations (Zephaniah 2:4–15).

Person of Christ in the book: The Just Lord (Zephaniah 3:5)

Portrait of the book: Prophecy

The Contents

I. **The Lord's determination in judgment** (Zephaniah 1:1–6)

 (a) Faithful justifier (Zephaniah 1:1)

(b) Fully judged (Zephaniah 1:2–4)

(c) Fairness judgment (Zephaniah 1:5–6)

II. **The Lord's day of judgment** (Zephaniah 1:7–3:8)

(a) People outlined here (Zephaniah 1:7–13)

(b) Period stated in the passage (Zephaniah 1:14–18)

(c) Places named in these chapters (Zephaniah 2:1–3:8)

III. **The Lord's deliverance based on justice** (Zephaniah 3:9–20)

(a) Regrouped people (Zephaniah 3:9–10)

(b) Repented people (Zephaniah 3:11–18)

(c) Redeemer's people (Zephaniah 3:19–20)

The Statistics

There are three chapters in Zephaniah, 53 verses, and 1, 617 words.

Conclusion

God had often proved to mankind that he is merciful and loving, he as well rebukes and disciplines at the same time. He pardons and receives the repentant. The Lord requires so little from us. Therefore, he has vowed to handle those who insist going after false gods. He promises to bless and be with those who seek after him. We should obey God and follow him with sincere hearts.

Haggai

Introduction

The book of Haggai is the second shortest book in the Hebrew Scripture. *Haggai* means "festive". This prophet is the only man with this name in the Old Testament. He was a prophet of Judah and ministered after the end of the Babylonian captivity. Haggai passed on his message to the governor of Judah, encouraging the rebuilding of the Temple. He assured that the future Temple would be more glorious than the previous one.

Prophet Haggai was solely concerned with the Temple that was destroyed during the siege. Fifteen years had passed; the returnees stayed in the Jewish community in Jerusalem with less concern about their place of worship. But Haggai's passionate preaching moved him to start and complete the Temple work despite opposition and different forms of discouragement. Haggai was the first of three prophets to preach after the return from exile, with only four months service.

The Book

Penman: Perhaps his parents gave him the name that means "festive" in hopes of future restoration of his people Israel. Or he may have been born on the Jewish holiday. This Babylonian-born Jew, Haggai, was the author of this book.

Person (s) addressed: The restored Jewish people

Period covered: This book was written around 520 BC, eighteen years after the return of the people to their homeland on 21 September of the second year of Darius' rule.

Position of the book in the Bible: Thirty-seventh book

Purpose of the book: As we all know, the Jewish Temple was the visible place where God and his people meet. In this case, ever since the people came back from Babylon, no one was concerned about the ruined Temple. For this reason, Haggai reminded them to put it in order because it was a symbol of God's presence.

Popular people in the book: Darius; Prophet Haggai; Zerubbabel, the governor; Joshua, the high priest

Places in the book: Babylon, Judah

Particular events in the book: luxurious houses and pockets with holes (Haggai 1:4–11), obedience attracts God's blessings (Haggai 2:10–19), Zerubbabel blessed (Haggai 2:20–23).

Person of Christ in the book: Lord Almighty (Haggai 2:23)

Portrait of the book: Prophecy and history

The Contents

I. **A caution to build the Temple** (Haggai 1)

(a) The background of Haggai's message (Haggai 1:1–2)

(b) The burden of Haggai's message (Haggai 1:3–11)

(c) The blessing of Haggai's message (Haggai 1:12–15)

II. **A call to behold the team** (Haggai 2:1–9)

(a) The present Temple reuse (Haggai 2:1–3)

(b) The partnership renewal (Haggai 2:4–5)

(c) The peaceful recapitulation (Haggai 2:6–9)

III. **A cause to believe the task** (Haggai 2:10–23)

(a) The promised blessing (Haggai 2:10–19)

(b) The powerful boss (Haggai 2:20–22)

(c) The prince beloved (Haggai 2:23)

The Statistics

There are two chapters in Haggai, 38 verses, and 1, 131 words.

Conclusion

This is the builder's book. Haggai drew his people's attention to the first priority in life. He called them to first build God's house—the Temple—before investing in their personal business. The first priority in life is God. Some take care of their physical needs without thinking of their spiritual lives. There should be a balance. Do not do anything on your own but acknowledge God. Our obedience must be complete.

Zechariah

Introduction

Zechariah means "Jehovah remembers". Prophet Zechariah properly identifies himself by his family root. He was the son of Berechiah, the son of Iddo. *Berechiah* means "Jehovah blesses", and *Iddo* means "the appointed time". Their names read thus: God remembers and blesses in the appointed time. Iddo (Nehemiah 12:4, 16) was one of the priests who came back from exile. The meaning of his name is a reminder that God has not forgotten his covenant with the founding fathers of the Jews. The Greek and Latin version of Zechariah's name is Zacharias.

Probably Zechariah was a Babylonian-born Jew, a prophet and priest from Judah joined with Haggai to encourage the new Jewish community to rebuild the Temple and return to the Lord. This most-quoted book in the New Testament is so fascinating. Zechariah also urged the people to live righteous lives with a promise that God would forgive those who turned to him in repentance, although sin must be punished. He ministered alongside Haggai for at least three more years after the end of the latter's ministry, which lasted only four months.

Zechariah commenced his work with eight visions using highly graphic language, and concluded with prophecies about the Jewish Messiah, Jesus Christ, the only hope of Israel's future, establishing his lasting kingdom.

The Book

Penman: Zechariah is the same name as the New Testament Greek Zacharias and English Zachary. Several men go by this name in the Old Testament. He was among the first group of individuals to return to Judah.

Person (s) addressed: Restored Jewish community

Period covered: About 520 BC, eighteen years after the captivity

Position of the book in the Bible: Thirty-eighth book

Purpose of the book: The freed captive Jews who had already begun the rebuilding of the Temple were greatly motivated and encouraged to continue the good work. Zechariah revealed to them God's bright and good future, which he had prepared for his people Israel. That alone gave them a sense of belonging and satisfaction.

Popular people in the book: Zechariah, Joshua, Darius, Berechiah, Iddo

Places in the book: Mount Olives, Jerusalem, Lebanon

Particular events in the book: king of Zion's coming (Zechariah 9:9–17), the reign of the Lord (Zechariah 14:1–21).

Person of Christ in the book: The Branch (Zechariah 3:8; 6:2)

Portrait of the book: Prophecy

The Contents

I. **The future of Israel as a nation** (Zechariah 1–6)

(a) Zechariah's appeal to Israel to change their minds (Zechariah 1:1–6)

(b) Zechariah's assorted visions for Israel's future (Zechariah 1:7–6:8)

(c) Zechariah assigned crown to Joshua as high priest (Zechariah 6:9–15)

II. **The fast of Israel as a nation** (Zechariah 7–8)

(a) Quest relating to fast acquired (Zechariah 7:1–3)

(b) Quest relating to fast argued (Zechariah 7:4–14)

(c) Quest relating to fast answered (Zechariah 8:1–23)

III. **The foolishness of Israel as a nation** (Zechariah 9–14)

(a) Coming and calling of the king sighted (Zechariah 9:1–10:12)

(b) Crucifixion and curse of the king settled (Zechariah 11:1–12:14)

(c) Compassion and coronation of the king stressed (Zechariah 13:1–14:21)

The Statistics

There are fourteen chapters in Zechariah, 211 verses, and 6, 444 words.

Conclusion

Zechariah ministered faithfully for the Lord and persuaded the people to give ears to God's word. He gave them the good news that God is still interested and had not finished with them. Their joy in the news of the long-awaited messiah's coming resulted in their surrender. This prophet outlined God's program for them as follows: God's watchful care over them; God's anger against Israel's enemies; an issue of New Jerusalem, purging of God's people's iniquity; God's power in action; God's holiness; and God as the overall ruler. What a great hope! To know that God is on your side—is that not wonderful?

Malachi

Introduction

Malachi means "messenger". Early Church fathers assumed that the writer of this book was an angel because both words have the same Greek meaning. Some suggest it is not a real name but simply an appellation for the revelation.

Malachi was a genuine prophet sent to address the new Jewish community that had finally settled in their own land. The city wall and Temple were in place, and many years had elapsed. Unfortunately, these freed captives did not learn enough from their past. Their sins had led them into slavery, and now they were doing the same thing all over again. There was a misuse of the Temple, corruption in the priesthood, marriage with heathens, and neglect of offering and tithe. God was displeased with the people and disappointed in them. Along with Haggai and Zechariah, Malachi called the people to their covenant relationship with the Lord.

Malachi ended his message as the last Old Testament book and prophet, anticipating that great God, the only saviour of humankind, Israel's coming Messiah. This book ends the Old Testament, and the New Testament begins following the intertestamental period.

The Book

Penman: Tradition has it that Malachi was a member of the great synagogue organized by Nehemiah, the governor. He was a Levite from the tribe of Zebulun who apparently condemned insincerity and hypocrisy.

Person (s) addressed: Restored Jews

Period covered: Written probably between 460 and 450 BC

Position of the book in the Bible: Thirty-ninth book

Purpose of the book: Malachi wants to show how the new community of Jews who came back from Babylon to Judah after many years of slavery had quickly forgotten. He examined why they had been punished before and why they had started living again in their old way. He warned them to return to God and do that which is right in God's sight. He made Israel realize that God has perpetually chosen to love them forever, so they should remain in his covenant.

Popular people in the book: Malachi, the priests, Judean citizens

Places in the book: Judah, Israel, Jerusalem

Particular events in the book: The Lord's promise of mercy to the people (Malachi 3:16–18), the Sun of Righteousness (Malachi 4:2).

Person of Christ in the book: The Sun of Righteousness (Malachi 4:2)

Portrait of the book: Prophecy

The Contents

I. **The Lord's comment concerning their sudden summit** (Malachi 1)

(a) God's love denied by the people (Malachi 1:1–5)

(b) God's name despised by the people (Malachi 1:6)

(c) God's alter defiled by the people (Malachi 1:7–14)

II. **The Lord's complaints concerning their specific sins** (Malachi 2)

(a) Priests worldliness disallowed (Malachi 2:1–9)

(b) Polluted worship described (Malachi 2:10–13)

(c) Prohibited wives dismissed (Malachi 2:14–17)

III. **The Lord's coming concerns sinners and saints** (Malachi 3:1–4:6)

(a) Servant's message heard (Malachi 3:1–18)

(b) Sinner's miserable hamartia (Malachi 4:1)

(c) Saints' messiah heralds (Malachi 4:2–6)

The Statistics

There are four chapters in Malachi, 55 verses, and 1, 782 words.

Conclusion

From the time of Adam and his wife until Malachi's time, and until now, God had been and will always demand our best—nothing less than that. As long as we show loyalty to him, he will go on blessing us. But those who rebel against his word are surely going to be punished without mercy. It is only humankind who change, not God. Trust him.

Part 2: Greek Scripture

Greek Scripture

This is the second cardinal segment of the Christian Scriptural canon. The New Testament, I strongly believe, is God's best story. He alone personally endeavours to save the lost, sinful human beings, and Scripture summarily directs everyone's attention to Jesus Christ, who manifested into the world to destroy the works of Satan so that humankind could be redeemed from all sin. Jesus paid the price in full of all our unrighteousness. We receive forgiveness for his sake. This is the entire message of the New Testament Scripture.

The New Testament books are twenty-seven in number: Matthew, Mark, Luke, John, Acts, Romans, 1 Corinthians, 2 Corinthians, Galatians, Ephesians, Philippians, Colossians, 1 Thessalonians, 2 Thessalonians, 1 Timothy, 2 Timothy, Titus, Philemon, Hebrews, James, 1 Peter, 2 Peter, 1 John, 2 John, 3 John, Jude, and Revelation.

Chapter 5

The Gospels

The first four books in the New Testament are the Gospels, and they tell the story of Jesus Christ, each different in its presentation according to the style of the writer. These books record Jesus's birth, life, death, and resurrection. The French nationalist Renan remarked, "The Gospel is the most beautiful book in the world" (Powell 1989, 1). These books consist of, Matthew, Mark, Luke, and John.

Matthew

Introduction

Little is known about Matthew except what we can learn from his Gospel. Tradition has it that he witnessed to the people of Ethiopia and later died a Christian martyr. One little detail is mentioned by Clement is that: "The Apostle Matthew partook of seeds, nuts, and vegetables, without flesh-meat" (Ward 1956, 53–54).

Matthew was a Jewish man employed by Rome as a tax collector. The publicans during Levi's era could assign an inflated value to the items being taxed, as a result, raising the taxes of a person. This practice was widespread, and most publicans became wealthy from the extra revenue. It is for this purpose that Jews looked at the job and individuals involved in it as dirty. Publicans were outcasts and traitors. In the midst of this job, Matthew became follower of Jesus Christ, the Jewish awaited Messiah, the greatest man who ever lived and God in the flesh.

Matthew's book brings the Jewish Bible and the New Testament books together. He quoted a lot from the Old Testament as sure proof that Jesus is the Messiah. *Matthew* means "gift of the Lord". He records almost every aspect of Christ's life. For instance, Matthew traces Christ's roots through to his resurrection; he reported and exposed the chief priests, elders, soldiers, and their corrupt minds and stubborn hearts when they bribed them at the resurrection (Matthew 28:11–15). Matthew concludes with Christ's last charge to his disciples to go and make him known to the whole world.

The Book

Penman: Matthew, whose name initially may have been Matthias, was probably the writer of the Gospel that carries his name. He is one of the apostles (Matthew 10:3; Mark 3:18; Luke. 6:15; Acts: 1:13) and is also known as Levi the publican whom Jesus called in Mark 2:14. Most scholars think that Matthias took on a new name, Matthew, when he gave up his former occupation (Demaray 1964, 134). Whether this is true or not should not create any disagreement over the content of the book.

Person (s) addressed: Jews

Period covered: Between AD 75 and 90

Position of the book in the Bible: Fortieth book

Purpose of the book: Matthew's primary objective was to prove to his fellow Jews that Jesus the has finally arrived, who was a descendant of Abraham and David.

Popular people in the book: Jesus Christ; the apostles; Jesus' Mother, Mary; Joseph the carpenter; Pontius Pilate, the governor; the wise men; Caiaphas, Joseph of Arimathea; King Herod; Simon of Cyrene; Barabbas

Places in the book: Bethlehem, Egypt, Jerusalem, Bethphage, Temple

Particular events in the book: the book of generations (Matthew 1:1–17), a virgin with a child (Matthew 1:18–25), visit of the wise men (Matthew 2:1–11), fearing God rather than the king (Matthew 2:12–15), Herod murdered children for political reasons, Herod's death and a Nazarene (Matthew 2:16–23), John's baptism of repentance (Matthew 3:1–12), Jesus's baptism and a voice from heaven (Matthew 3:13–17), Jesus's temptation (Matthew 4:1–11), John in prison (Matthew 4:12–16), Jesus's message (Matthew 4:17), busy men called (Matthew 4:18–22), Jesus's three-fold ministry (Matthew 4:23), great multitude followed him (Matthew 4:24–25), the great Sermon on the Mount known as the Beatitudes (Matthew chapters 5, 6, and 7), a leper healed (Matthew 8:1–4), a recommended faith (Matthew 8:5–13), Peter's mother-in-law's sickness (Matthew 8:14–17), Jesus the healer (Matthew 9:1–38), the twelve were commissioned (Matthew 10:1–42), John sent two messengers to Christ from prison with a question (Matthew 11:1–6), laborers are invited (Matthew 11:28–30), the called him names (Matthew 11:16–19; 27:63), Jesus referred to Sodom (Matthew 11:20–24), the sign of Jonah is enough (Matthew 12:38–45), Jesus's true mother, brother, and sister (Matthew 12:46–50), when men sleep (Matthew 13:24–30), chapter of various parables (Matthew 13:1–52), Jesus in his own town (Matthew 13:53–58), reason for John's imprisonment (Matthew 14:1–12), Jesus's compassion, Jesus fed the multitude with five loaves and two fishes (Matthew 14:13–21), a personal private prayer encouraged, Peter saved from sinking and doubt (Matthew 14:22–33), all that were diseased made whole (Matthew 14:34–36), upon the confession of Peter (Matthew 16:13–20), the transfiguration (Matthew 17:1–10), cursed fig tree (Matthew 21:17–22), woes on the blind guards (Matthew 23:1–39), signs of the last days and warnings (Matthew 24:1–51), the ten virgins (Matthew 25:1–13), plans to decimate Jesus (Matthew 26:1–16), Judas Iscariot is the one (Matthew 26:17–25), Peter's boast (Matthew 26:26–35), Peter's mistake corrected (Matthew 26:69–75), Christ arrested and handed over to Pontius Pilate, Judas Iscariot's thirty pieces of silver and the field of blood (Matthew 27:1–31), crucifixion and death (Matthew 27:32–50), many things took place when he gave up the ghost (Matthew 27:51–56), Jesus was buried (Matthew 27:57–61), guards at the tomb (Matthew 27:62–65), living Christ (Matthew 28:1–10), unacceptable soldiers' report (Matthew 28:11–15), the empowered followers (Matthew 28:16–20).

Person of Christ in the book: King of the Jews (Matthew 27:11)

Portrait of the book: History

The Contents

I. **The revealed promised potentate** (Matthew 1–10)

(a) Personality profile of the awaited king (Matthew 1:1–4:11)

(b) Particular purpose of the awaited king (Matthew 4:12–7:29)

(c) Precious power of the awaited king (Matthew 8:1–10–42)

II. **The rejected passionate potentate** (Matthew 11:1–27:66)

(a) Facing the foes (Matthew 11:1–12:50)

(b) Followers thoroughly formed (Matthew 13:1–23:39)

(c) Foretells of the future (Matthew 24:1–27–66)

III. **The risen proficient potentate** (Matthew 28)

(a) Joyful message angelic light (Matthew 28:1–10)

(b) Jews madness absolute lie (Matthew 28:11–15)

(c) Joining meritorious a real lord (Matthew 28:16–20)

The Statistics

There are twenty-eight chapters in Matthew, 1, 071 verses, and 23, 684 words.

Conclusion

The Gospel of Matthew is the most complete record of Christ's teachings and was written to convince Jews everywhere that Jesus was the one promised by the prophets in the Jewish Scripture, the Old Testament. There was a common belief among the Jews that a day was coming on which the Messiah would become a powerful military leader who would rise against the Roman occupation. Instead of this, Jesus told them his kingdom was not of this world. No wonder Matthew the Gospel spreader emphasised the Lord's word concerning the kingdom of heaven.

What is your view regarding the Messiah who has come? Do not tell me your answer. Of course, I feel you have something to say. He came to save us from sin and Satan. He is not only Messiah to the Jews but to all people, Jews and Gentiles alike. Have you been saved by him? Jesus desires us to trust him while we live here on earth, and he has given us instructions on how to serve him better as our only king now and forever.

Mark

Introduction

John Mark was the son of Mary and a cousin of Barnabas (Colossians 4:10). He, at first, was a member of Paul's traveling team until a difference of opinion parted them (Acts 15:37). Mark's Hebrew name was John, and his Roman name, Marcus. His name means "defence" ("hammer"). John Mark is mentioned several times in the New Testament, with both names used, and five times as Mark. He is not one of the original apostles; perhaps he turned out to be a personal and trusted friend of Peter. He was an active member of Peter's audience in Rome, which meant that, after the death of the apostle in AD 65, he supposedly used the documents of Peter that recorded Jesus's words. This was the primary reference for his work (Hymer and Bullen 1971, 85). There is the assumption that Mark must have received most of his information from the apostle. This earliest gospel is the shortest of the gospels yet presents Jesus as the anointed (Messiah) Christ, the mighty worker rather than a great teacher.

Mark's general theme is the person of Jesus Christ. It is the story Peter told and Mark recorded. Justin Martyr spoke of Mark's Gospel as Peter's Memoir (Hymer and Bullen 1971, 108); Papias, one of the early Christian leaders, described the Gospel in these words: "Mark, indeed, who became the interpreter of Peter, wrote accurately, as far as he remembered them, the things said or done by the Lord, but not however in order. For he had neither heard the Lord nor been his personal follower, but at a later stage, as I said, he had followed Peter who used to adapt his teaching to the need {of the time} but not as though he were drawing up a connected account" (Hymer and Bullen 1971, 85). Mark explained in great detail Christ's ministry of the perfect servant from his baptism to his resurrection. He addressed both Jews and Gentiles, and specifically a Roman audience, proving that Jesus indeed was what he claimed to be. The Gospel of Mark is similar in content to the Gospels of Matthew and Luke. It's one of the synoptic gospels.

The Book

Penman: Mark's mother was a Jerusalem resident and house owner. The early disciples used her property as place of worship and meeting (Acts 12:12). Mark was a youthful convert and disciple of Apostle Paul; he was also secretary and disciple of Apostle Peter (Acts 12:12, 25; 13:5; Colossians 4:10; 2 Timothy 4:11; 1 Peter 5:13) (Dicharry 1991, 35). He penned the book single headedly with no unnecessary argument.

Person (s) addressed: The Gospel of Mark seems to be written in Rome for the community of faith there, including those who joined from Judaism as well as from pagan religions. This historical tradition has numerous supports from the evangelist's work. Evidence that Gentiles were among the readers comes from this preacher elucidating the custom of the Jew in Mark 7:3.

Maybe another argument that Mark aimed at Roman readers is the elucidation of a Greek by a Latin one in Mark 12:42. Mark used nine "latinisms" (*denarius*; *census*; *quadrans*; *grabatum* for "bed" five times; *legion*; *centurion*; *sextarius* for a measure translated as "pot" in Mark 7:4; *speculator* for soldier in Mark 6:27; the Latin turn of phrase translated as "satisfy" in Mark 15:15). But only the final four of these are right to the evangelist, and almost all the nine have been discovered to have been in general used in the Mediterranean world at the time (Jones 1963, 55). Jews and non-Jews were his audience.

Period covered: This is the earliest of the Gospels. We know this because Matthew and Luke used Mark as a source. Mark was written approximately AD 65–75.

Position of the book in the Bible: Forty-first book

Purpose of the book: Mark explained who Jesus was to the Romans who wanted to know more about this great worker by showing them some practical works he performed which had never occurred before or after the Roman power.

Popular people in the book: Jesus, John the Baptist, Peter, James, Herod, Pontius Pilate, chief priests, Judas Iscariot

Places in the book: Desert, large upper room, Garden of Gethsemane, sepulchre

Particular events in the book: John the Baptist prepared the way (Mark 1:1–8), Jesus's baptism (Mark 1:9–11), Christ the healer (Mark 1:29–34), Jesus's rejection in Nazareth (Mark 6:1–6), feeding of the five thousand (Mark 6:30–46), Jesus predicted his death (Mark 8:31–38), the transfiguration (Mark 9:1–14), the triumphal entry (Mark 11:1–14), thieves in the Temple (Mark 11:15–19), two mites (Mark 12:41–44), burial of Jesus (Mark 15:42–47, the resurrection (Mark 16:1–20).

Person of Christ in the book: The Perfect Servant of God (Mark 10:45)

Portrait of the book: History

The Contents

I. **The perfect servant and his call** (Mark 1:1–8:26)

(a) His work (Mark 1:1–3:35)

(b) His words (Mark 4:1–5:43)

(c) His ways (Mark 6:1–8:26)

II. **The perfect servant and his colleagues** (Mark 8:27–10:52)

(a) Testimony and discipleship (Mark 8:27–38)

(b) Transfiguration and disputation (Mark 9:1–50)

(c) Teachings and details (Mark 10:1–52)

III. **The perfect servant and his cross** (Mark 11–16)

(a) Master's purpose and parables (Mark 11:1–13:37)

(b) Master's Passover and problems (Mark 14:1–15:47)

(c) Master's power and proclamation (Mark 16:1–20)

The Statistics

There are sixteen chapters in Mark, 678 verses, and 15, 171 words.

Conclusion

This young disciple once accompanied Apostles Paul and Barnabas on their first missionary trips, but when he refused to join them on the second journey, a row resulted between them. Mark probably acted as an interpreter for Apostle Peter as he ministered to Greek and Latin listeners. Never run away from suffering for Christ. Some disciples died during Emperor Nero's persecution. Nero claimed that Christians burned Rome; he used them as scapegoats in order to direct people's attention away from his atrocities. Still, Mark informs us of the great power of Jesus at work by his many miracles.

Jesus came into the world only to die for our many sins with no exception. For this reason, God demands that we must turn away from those evil deeds and accept his only Son who suffered and died to bring us back to God.

Luke

Introduction

Luke, the Christian doctor and second-generation Christian, was a very close friend and companion of Apostle Paul. Luke is the only book in the New Testament penned by a Gentile believer at the time when Greeks were looking for a perfect divine human being—one with the best characteristics of both man and woman but none was without shortcomings. "Luke the physician," one of the Church fathers, Jerome, comments, "by leaving us his Gospel and his Acts of the apostles has shown us how the apostles became from fishers of fish to fishers of men; for he himself became a physician of the body to a physician of the soul ... As often as his book is read in the Church, so often does his medicine flow out" (Ward 1956, 129).

A native of Antioch of Syria, Luke, whose name means "light giving", was highly educated and was to write his gospel in good Greek style. He was also the author of the book of Acts. Some have said he may have gone to the nearest university for his medical training, and that would be in Tarsus since Antioch of Syria, his hometown, was not too far. It is further suggested that the young physician embraced faith in Christ while a student, being influenced by Saul of Tarsus.

Dr Luke, a good Bible student, clearly took time to investigate and document the most total episode of the earthly life and work of Jesus, which had not been penned by the other evangelists. He extensively showed the human nature of Jesus and his place in history. As Stephen Miller put it: "Jesus is humanity's saviour, Matthew and Mark don't even use the word 'saviour' but John uses it once, Luke thought to be non-Jewish, carefully selects stories that show salvation is for everyone - not just the Jews: 'I have seen the saviour ... given to all people. He is a light to reveal God to the nations'" (Luke 2:30–32) (Miller 2006, 90). Therefore, Luke gave us a record of Christ's virgin birth and presented him as the universal saviour, the compassionate healer and teacher. Luke stressed further the Holy Spirit power in the life of Jesus as well as his prayer life. Finally, Luke confirmed without doubt that Matthew's gospel directly pointed to the Jews. Mark primarily addressed the Romans while Luke focused on the Greeks.

The Book

Penman: There are different opinions as to who the penman was; this has been a long-time issue. The early Church fathers (Clement of Alexandria, Justin Martyr, Hegesippus, Irenaeus, Tertullian, and the Muratorian Canon) all believed Luke to have written this informative gospel. Jewish tradition also attests and affirms that physician Luke was the writer.

Person (s) addressed: The gospel was addressed to Theophilus, whose name means "friend of God". Some say that this unknown man may have been a Roman official. Others believe he was a Gentile community leader. Obviously, he was a respected devout, pious, and committed Christian friend of Doctor Luke. Luke assured his dear friend that the faith he had embraced was built on a sure and strong foundation.

Period covered: If the book of Acts was really written before the destruction of Jerusalem in AD 70, then a date of AD 80 would be considered correct, though some assume otherwise.

Position of the book in the Bible: Forty-second book

Purpose of the book: Luke was intended to bring the attention of the general public to a comprehensive record of the historical life and ministry of the Lord Jesus Christ. The author claims that his audience should be thoroughly furnished with information and should continue to trust in him. Wilfrid Harrington calls this audience, "Christians who live in the post–apostolic age" (Harrington 1982, 33). I do believe him.

Popular people in the book: Jesus Christ; John the Baptist; Joseph; Mary; Peter; James; John the Beloved; the wise men; Pontius Pilate; Caiaphas; Elizabeth; Zechariah; Simeon; Anna; Lazarus; Mary, the sister of Martha; Zacchaeus; Judas Iscariot

Places in the book: Galilee, Bethlehem, Nazareth, manger, Temple, Jerusalem, Bethphage, Bethany, Emmaus.

Particular events in the book: prophecy of Zechariah (Luke 1:67–80), the shepherds (Luke 2:8–24), prophecy of Simeon (Luke 2:25–35), Jesus's baptism (Luke 3:21–22) Roman officer's faith (Luke 7:1–10), sinful woman forgiven (Luke 7:36–50), women who love Jesus (Luke 8:1–3), Jesus real family (Luke 8:19–21), confusion of Herod (Luke 9:7–9), the feeding of five thousand (Luke 9:10–17), repentance demanded (Luke 13:1–5), ten lepers (Luke 17:11–19), persistent widow (Luke 18:1–8), valuable offering of a widow (Luke 21:1–4), Satan entered into Judas Iscariot (Luke 22:1–6), Jesus's death (Luke 23:44–55, rise and ascension (Luke 24:1–53).

Person of Christ in the book: The Perfect Son of Man (Luke 7:34)

Portrait of the book: History

The Contents

I. **Activities pointing to the coming of the perfect Son of Man** (Luke 1:1–4:13)

(a) The beginning and the birth of Christ (Luke 1:1–2:39)

 (b) The boyhood and the baptism of Christ (Luke 2:40–3:22)

(c) The background and the battle of Christ (Luke 3:23–4:13)

II. **Activities pointing to the career of the perfect Son of Man** (Luke 4:14–21:38)

(a) The Lord's work in Galilee (Luke 4:14–9:50)

(b) The Lord's way to Golgotha (Luke 9:51–20:47)

(c) The Lord's worth of greatness (Luke 21:1–38)

III. **Activities pointing to the Calvary of the perfect Son of Man** (Luke 22–24)

(a) The Lord's table and his tears (Luke 22:1–53)

(b) The Lord's trials and his tree (Luke 22:54–23:49)

(c) The Lord's tomb and his triumph (Luke 23:50–24:53)

The Statistics

There are twenty-four books in Luke, 1, 151 verses, and 25, 944 words.

Conclusion

Luke rightly traced Jesus's genealogy back to the first Adam (Luke 3:23–38) indicating that Jesus was truly born of a virgin mother, Mary, who was also of the flesh. Jesus was vividly depicted by the physician as a perfect human being in this beautiful writeup. Luke described in detail Jesus's gracious instructions, the vigorous actions of his fruitful activities, how the Lord ended his earthly work, died, and rose from the dead after three days as he had predicted. More importantly, Doctor Luke the evangelist taught that Jesus is the only hope for depraved humanity.

Looking at the message of Saint Luke in his book, we discover that Jesus is the only person who ever lived in the human body who never did any wrong throughout his lifetime. Luke pointed out Jesus's compassionate life——how he took care of everyone: women, men, children, weak widows, the homeless, hopeless individuals, the friendless, and so many others. The list is quite endless. Jesus meets every need at all times. Jesus's prayer life draws attention. He prays without stopping. While others—even his disciples—were in deep sleep, the man Jesus was busy praying. Luke intentionally penned this particular information about him so that we, with multiple needs in the world of pain, should earnestly pray day, night, and always. In reality, the writer was Jesus as God-man—the Son of Man and the Son of God! Go for Him.

John

Introduction

Here John the Beloved, not John the Baptist, is the subject. John means "Jehovah is gracious" or "favoured of Jehovah". In chapter 13:23, John is referred to as the disciple "whom Jesus loves". John was the son of Zebedee and a brother of James, another of the followers of Jesus Christ. James, along with Paul and some other disciples, died early during Nero's persecution as the emperor tried to use Christians as scapegoats to avoid taking the blame. John was the last apostle to receive death. Originally, these apostles were fishermen who worked along with their father as partners. They were successful businessmen until they joined Christ. John's mother, Salome, and Jesus's mother, Mary, were related.

Maisie Ward, remarks:

> Of all the Evangelists, John is the one we can know intimately and who yet, like the eagle that is his symbol, flies from us, his gaze fixed upon the sun. He is the most mystical of the evangelists, yet the most human too. We can never forget that his humanity is especially close to that of the Son of man: he was the loved by Jesus, and for many years he lived with Mary. It is not memory only, but this double companionship that makes his voice, of all the evangelists', the closet echo of his Lord's. (Ward 1956, 222)

John, a former disciple of John the Baptist, left him for Jesus after Jesus was introduced to them. Later he was chosen as one of the apostles so he could have a special relationship with Jesus. He was a member of inner circle who witnessed the events of the transfiguration on the mount. John saw Jesus raise the daughter of Jairus to life. He was an eyewitness to Jesus's supplication and suffering in the Garden of Gethsemane. He was the only apostle to witness Christ's crucifixion (John 19:26). John became a prominent figure in the Jerusalem Church. Roman authority compulsorily pushed him into the island of Patmos (the present dayTurkey) to die because of his faith.

As the first century came to an end, there arose many false teachers who supported all sorts of doctrines in the name of the gospel and the works of Christ, and the apostles were under threat. The purity and truth found in the Church was corrupted by these people. Then John, inspired by the Holy Spirit, wrote this work as a summary of what he had learned from his master (John 20:31). Only the gospel of John proved at least a three years of Christ's earthly ministry. The synoptic gospels seem to show that Jesus Christ's public ministry only lasted for one year.

Additionally, John concludes his gospel with useful information not seen elsewhere (John 21:1–25). The epilogue to this gospel was to make more vivid the responsibilities of the apostles and his relationship with them (Benware 1990, 136). Lastly, John's gospel is the book about communion and heavenly reflection. He is the only gospel writer who did not mention Christ's parables but particularly and constantly demonstrated Jesus as the manifestation of God.

The Book

Penman: There has been debate as to who wrote the gospel of Saint John. People like Clement of Alexandria, Justin Martyr, and Irenaeus, the early Church writers and most trusted leaders in the history of the Christian Church, said that the former fisherman and the beloved of Jesus Christ, John, was the author, and no other person. John closely walked with Jesus, and Polycarp served John while Irenaeus learned under the leadership of Polycarp. He was also the writer of four other books of the New Testament.

Person (s) addressed: All people (the world)

Period covered: It is likely to be around between AD 90 and 100.

Position of the book in the Bible: Forth-third book

Purpose of the book: John proposed to write this gospel to encourage men and women to believe that Jesus was the Son of God and in believing in him will provide eternal life for the believer (John 20:30–31). The apostle later cited the seven outstanding miracles to substantiate his facts. There is a call to believe and encourage our walk with Jesus.

Popular people in the book: Jesus Christ, disciples of Christ, John the Baptist, Mary, Joseph, Judas Iscariot, Elizabeth, Zechariah, Nathanael, Judean governor Pontius Pilate

Places in the book: River Jordan, Galilee, Temple, Samaria, Jerusalem, Pool of Bethesda, Pool of Siloam, Gabbatha (The day Pilate sentenced Jesus to death, he sat down on the judgment seat on the platform which is known as the "stone pavement" but in Hebrew it is called "Gabbatha" Golgotha [Hebrew] or skull hill.)

Particular events in the book: The Word is God (John 1:1–5), miracle wine (John 2:1–11), Jesus visits Capernaum (John 2:12), destroy this Temple (John 2:13–22), Jesus knew all men (John 2:23–25), Nicodemus, a Jewish ruler and his discussion with Jesus (John 3:1–13), the Bible's best verse (John 3:16), the woman with five husbands (John 4:1–29), search the Scriptures (John 5:39), the bread of life (John 6:35, 41, 48, 51), the light of the world (John 8:12; 9:5), the door (John 10:7,9), the Good Shepherd (John 10:11,14), Jews of late and the house of Lazarus (John 11:1–46), the resurrection and life (John 11:25), the way, the truth and the life (John 14:6), the vine (John 15:1, 5) Jesus meeting with a confused governor (John 18:28–40; 19:1–16), Barabbas was a robber (John 18:28–40), it is finished (John 19:30), Jesus was crucified (John 19:38–42), Jesus greeted Mary Magdalene (John 20:11–18), Jesus appeared to the disciples (John 20:19–31), Jesus said other things that are not written in the book of John (John 21:25).

Person of Christ in the book: The Perfect Son of God (John 19:7)

Portrait of the book: History

The Contents

I. **The signs of the perfect Son of God** (John 1:1–12:50)

(a) Christ's divinity described (John 1:1–4:54)

(b) Christ's divinity disapproved (John 5:1–10:42)

(c) Christ's divinity disentitled (John 11:1–12:50)

II. **The secrets of the perfect Son of God** (John 13–17)

(a) Practical lessons (John 13:1–38)

(b) Private lectures (John 14:1–16:33)

(c) Prayer legator (John 17:1–26)

III. **The sorrows of the perfect Son of God** (John 18–21)

(a) Falsely condemned by the Jews (John 18:1–19:15)

(b) Formally crucified by the soldiers (John 19:16–42)

(c) Faithfully conquered by the cross (John 20:1–21:25)

The Statistics

There are twenty-one chapters in John, 878 verses, and 19, 099 words.

Conclusion

John concludes that Jesus Christ was the Godman who is eternal and identical in essence with God. Christ's first year of ministry was recorded by John alone. For instance, the turning of the water into wine at the wedding ceremony in Cana was Jesus's first miracle (John 2:1–11). You remember the cleansing of the Temple, Jesus's meeting with Nicodemus by night, and Jesus's conversation with woman at the well.

The synoptic gospels recorded several great activities of Jesus's second year of ministry, but John devoted his time to discussing the life and work and teachings. He mentioned the bread of life that came down from heaven. He focused on Jesus's deity and special relationship with God that generated envy and an attack on Christ. John recorded Christ's final year—the Good Shepherd, the light of the world, and the resurrection of the life.

The night before Jesus's death was Passover. Jesus highlighted certain truths about the Holy Spirit, his Church, and his disciples' relationships with one another. Finally, he prayed for them to the Father during the few hours remaining. They all left the Upper Room for the Garden of Gethsemane where Judas Iscariot moved out of the band secretly to high priests and elders, which led to our Lord's arrest and crucifixion.

The Gospel of John is crucial and a "spiritual gospel". The gospel contains the best verse ever recognized in the entire New Testament. Martin Luther called John 3:16 "The Gospel in a nutshell". What a good book! Several lessons were given to us by John about God's only Son. He says that only in him is there salvation. Jesus must be acknowledged by everyone as he shows us what love is about and how we should love one another. Lastly, John proves to us that Jesus has total authority over Satan and his cohorts.

Chapter 6

The New Testament Historical Book

There is only one book of history in the New Testament. It tells story about the first century Christian Church with special emphasis on the ministries of Peter and Paul, who are outstanding figures of the first and later chapters of the book. The book also records events of the Day of Pentecost, how the Church began, the accurate power of the Holy Ghost, the return of Christ to heaven, his program for the Church, the persecution and progress of the early Church. This book of history is the Acts of the Apostles.

Acts

Introduction

Acts of the Apostles is the best book known in the world that ever existed that could clearly teach you everything you need to understand about the birth, infancy, persecution, and growth of the founder of the Christian Church. Without this book, we would have, perhaps, remained in darkness not knowing where to go regarding the Church.

Having spent many years studying Scriptures, J. B. Philips has this to say concerning Acts as been quoted by William McDonald when he says that in no comparable period of human history has "any small body of ordinary people so moved the world that their enemies could say, with tears of rage in their eyes, that these men 'have turned the world upside down!'" (MacDonald 1995, 1576). We should not consider Acts a doctrinal book; instead, we should view it as a historical book. It gives us detailed information concerning the Church of Christ with clarity.

Right from the inception of the book through to the end, the Holy Spirit is so powerful that the gospel is able to begin from Jerusalem and travel rapidly to Rome. Nothing would have been responsible or achieved if Jesus was not there. The book covers a time of approximately thirty-three years but revolves around three pioneers: Simon, also called Peter; Stephen, the first martyr; and Saul of Tarsus. It starts with the Jews but finishes with Gentiles. The book should have been called Acts of the Holy Spirit instead of Acts of the Apostles because the Holy Spirit is mentioned about fifty-eight times in the twenty-eight chapters (Philips 1987, 170–171).

In the first part of Acts, Peter is the leading figure. He spoke under the anointing of the Spirit on that great day of Pentecost, which resulted in three thousand being brought to the kingdom. In the second segment of the book, Apostle Paul is prominent. His missionary trips are traced, and several churches were established in foreign and virgin soils. The gospel is promoted and proclaimed, and Christ is witnessed. This is proper comprehensive information from that physician, the beloved Luke.

The Book

Penman: Several Church fathers (see Luke's introduction) and even tradition concur that Luke, who authored the gospel of Luke, is the same person who wrote the book of Acts (Colossians 4:14). Take your time to find out the medical words used in Acts. I suppose it might be the work of a physician like Luke (Acts 3:7; 9:18, 33; 13:11; 20:8–10).

Person (s) addressed: Theophilus, a Gentile convert and physician Luke's personal friend

Period covered: Most Bible students may not bother collecting the dates of some New Testament books, but when it comes to the book of Acts, we should pay attention to the date because it specifically deals with the Christian Church and demands attention. This date is essential. It is about AD 63–64.

Position of the book in the Bible: Forth-fourth book

Purpose of the book: Luke intends to inform his fellow dear Gentile friend, Theophilus. He had earlier written Theophilus about Jesus's preaching and teaching. In Acts, Luke intended to continue documenting Jesus and his followers. Working under the direction of God's Holy Spirit, Luke explained how Jesus's words had rapidly reached the whole world and made a strong impact.

Popular people in the book: According to John Philips, the book is in three parts, each with different emphasis. The first describes God's man, Simon Peter. The second is about God's Martyr, Stephen. And the third displays God's missionary, Saul (Philips 2001, 190). However, I do add to the list the following; a fourth part demonstrates God's mercy in the story of Barnabas. And the fifth describes God's mouth, Matthias.

Places in the book: Jerusalem, Judea, Samaria, Rome, the Beautiful Gate, Aceldama, Antioch, Thessalonica, Philippi, Ephesus, Tarsus, Caesarea, Amphipolis, Apollonia, Berea

Particular events in the book: the man who replaced Judas Iscariot (Acts 1:20–26), meeting of Christians only (Acts 2:43–47), crippled healed (Acts 3:1–11), Peter and John with the council (Acts 4:1–37), lying couples (Acts 5:1–11), seven chosen men (Acts 6:1–15), Stephen's long address and his death (Acts 7:1–60), Ethiopian eunuch (Acts 8:1–40), conversion of the adamant, zealous, and pious Pharisee, Saul (Acts 9:1–31), Aeneas and Dorcas (Acts 9:32–43), James killed, but Peter escaped (Acts 12:1–19), nature of Herod Agrippa's death (Acts 12:20–25), church at Antioch (Acts 13:1–3), Bar–Jesus (Acts 13:4–13), epistles to Gentile Christians (Acts 15:1–35), division over John Mark between Paul and his good friend, Barnabas (Acts 15:36–41), Paul and Silas—Roman citizens (Acts 16:1–40), council of philosophers (Acts 17:16–34), deportation of Aquila and his wife, Priscilla (Acts 18:1–28), twelve men with John's baptism (Acts 19:1–7), school of Tyrannus (Acts 19:8–12), a team of Jewish vagabonds (Acts 19:13–20), plot against Paul (Acts 23:12–22), Paul appears before Felix, Festus, and Agrippa (Acts chapters 24, 25, 26), Paul's warning on the ship (Acts 27:1–44), father of Publius healed and Paul in Roman land with the Gospel (Acts 28:1–31).

Person of Christ in the book: Ascended Lord (Acts 1:9)

Portrait of the book: History

The Contents

I. **The famous foundation of the Christian Church** (Acts 1–5)

(a) Preparation of the work (Acts 1:1–2:47)

(b) Persecution against the work (Acts 3:1–4:30)

(c) Progression of the work (Acts 4:31:5:42)

II. **The firm faithfulness of the Christian Church** (Acts 6–12)

(a) Several voices (Acts 6:1–8:50)

(b) Startling victories (Acts 9:1–11:30)

(c) Stirring violence (Acts 12:1–25)

III. **The foreign field of the Christian Church** (Acts 13–28)

(a) Paul the prophet (Acts 13:1–3)

(b) Paul the pioneer (Acts 13:4–21:26)

(c) Paul the prisoner (Acts 21:27–28:31)

The Statistics

There are twenty-eight chapter in Acts, 1, 007 verses, and 24, 250 words.

Conclusion

I have mentioned earlier that someone has suggested that the book of Acts should have been titled The Acts of the Holy Spirit. This may be the result of the Spirit's presence and power throughout the book. Luke, in Acts, teaches us that the message about Jesus Christ must be shared with everyone since only in Christ's name can we receive a blissful, durable, and quality life. Programmes and plans offered by our various local churches do not yield much fruit in terms of growing the Body of Christ without the aid of the Spirit. Let us allow the Holy Spirit of God to work in our lives and assemblies.

Chapter 7

Doctrinal Epistles

The doctrinal books are the epistles or letters written by Apostle Paul; there are thirteen in number. These books are so important to the Church's life and should not be treated lightly as some do today. Someone refers them as books written based on circs and that should not be reckoned as doctrinal books. This theory to me seems unfounded.

Doctrinal books elucidate the way Christians should live. They present the true pattern of worship and are an appeal to continue in Christ's Word until he returns. After the end of the world, God's judgment will follow. Everyone's deeds at last shall be rewarded whether good or evil. The doctrinal books, for the sake of this work, are divided into three groups: personal, prison, and pastoral letters.

The personal letters are Romans, 1 Corinthians, 2 Corinthians, 1 Thessalonians, 2 Thessalonians, and Galatians. In these books, encouragement is given to the recipients, several questions answered, and other significant matters relating to the Christian faith, past, present and future are treated.

The prison letters are Ephesians, Philippians, Colossians, and Philemon. Apostle Paul wrote these books while in his Roman prison.

The pastoral letters are 1 Timothy, 2 Timothy, and Titus. Because they are addressed to young pastors, these books are commonly referred to as pastoral epistles. Subject matter includes the pastoral care of God's people and the exercises of the pastoral office, such as Christian living, doctrine, leadership, and the life of the Church in general.

Romans

Introduction

Romans is one of the Pauline epistles. It is the longest, most influential, and vital of all the Bible books. The book provides a fundamental statement to Christian thought. The Church in Rome received this letter from Apostle Paul who had never visited but desired to do so. He wrote from Corinth on his third missionary trip about twenty–five years later. You may not know reason the writer pointed to every truth of the gospel in his Romans' letter.

In the world at that time, Roman emperors were considered as gods by citizens. To stand as a Christian in such environment required nothing but the whole truth and courage, so being a believer in Rome would not be simple or something to be taken lightly. This local assembly was totally a mixed congregation. The founders of this local denomination were probably those visitors in Jerusalem on the Day of Pentecost (Acts 2). Neither Peter nor Paul founded the Church, which is opposite to public opinions.

In his summation of the Christian teaching, Paul explained what the Gospel is all about, indicating to them that all have sinned yet a way of escape has been provided; he educated the Roman Christians, telling them how God had not completely forgotten the Jews and their future hope. He thoroughly informed them concerning daily living as believers in Christ in an ungodly society.

The Book

Penman: Apostle Paul

Person (s) addressed: The Christians in Rome

Period covered: Approximately AD 55 to 57. The book is among the Pauline epistles written after 1 and 2 Corinthians; it takes place at the end of Paul's third missionary journey. He stayed at Corinth for three months.

Position of the book in the Bible: Forty-fifth book

Purpose of the book: Paul's intention for writing, apart from his sincere desire to visit the Christians in Rome, was to challenge and encourage them in the fundamental truth of the Gospel, and most importantly to present to the Roman citizens the same crucified Jesus who had become the only means by which people could make peace with God. He affirmed that living without him on earth attracts God's terrible anger.

Popular people in the book: Paul, Priscilla, Aquila, Phebe, Rufus, Timothy, Jason

Places in the book: Corinth, Cenchrea, Rome

Particular events in the book: God's wrath at sin (Romans 1:1–32), all with no exception has sinned (Romans 3:1–31), joy follows faith (Romans 5:11), power of sin broken (Romans 6:23), life in spirit (Romans 8:1–39), Israel's nation chosen (Romans 9:1–33), God's mercy for all people (Romans 11:1–36), lists of faithful friends (Romans 16:1–27).

Person of Christ in the book: Our Righteousness (Romans 5:21)

Portrait of the book: Doctrine

The Contents

I. **The principles of Christianity: relating to the Gospel** (Romans 1–8)

(a) Questions about sin (Romans 1:1–3:20)

(b) Questions about salvation (Romans 3:21–5:21)

(c) Questions about sanctification (Romans 6:1–8:39)

II. **The problem of Christianity: relating to the Jews** (Romans 9–11)

(a) Past of Israel's nation (Romans 9:1–33)

(b) Present of Israel's nation (Romans 10:1–21)

(c) Promise of Israel's nation (Romans 11:1–36)

III. **The practice of Christianity: Relating to practical living** (Romans 12–16)

(a) Laws of Christian life (Romans 12:1–13:7)

(b) Learners of Christian love (Romans 13:8–16:24)

(c) Lord of Christian light (Romans 16:25–27)

The Statistics

There are sixteen chapters in Romans, 433 verses, and 9, 447 words.

Conclusion

The book of Romans is a complete handbook for apologetics. It contains all doctrines of the Scripture without anything lacking. Its didactic covers humanity's fall in Genesis to humanity's restoration. In between the two books, Jesus in the middle solves man's problem. The theological nature of Romans through ages, even in the era of Church fathers, drew attention. For instance, in AD 380, Augustine became a Christian after reading Romans 13:13–14. Martin Luther in AD 1517 is said to have understood the phrase "the just shall live by faith" from the book, and that changed the course of history. The founder of the Methodist church, John Wesley, according to history received assurance of salvation by hearing the preface to Martin's commentary on Romans read in a Moravian House church on Aqidersgate Street in London in 1738. Furthermore, John Muir (1838–1914) called it, "The Book of Nature". And Calvin wrote, "When anyone understands this Epistle, he has a passage opened to him to the understanding of the whole Scripture."

Personally, I look at this book as the heart of the Gospel. In it we have the God of grace and love who waits for sinners to come home. Paul extensively tells us about the Lord Jesus Christ, the only mediator, a true sacrifice for our atonement. The epistle does not come to a close without teaching us how to live to the glory of God so that we can be happy people in whom God delights and of whom he can be proud of.

1 Corinthians

A young congregation was just being planted by the apostle Paul in his third preaching tour in the busy city of Corinth about two years before the writing of this epistle, while he was still in Ephesus (Acts 18:1–9). Corinth was in the southern part of Greece. It was a wealthy city but corrupt; it became known as centre for international trading routes. Its seaports drew people from all walks of life. In this city was the temple of Aphrodite, the goddess of love. Located on the top of the Acrocorinth (the Acropolis of ancient Corinth), the temple housed one thousand sacred prostitutes who were to help in the worship of Aphrodite, the Greek name for Venus. Several other temples were built in various locations of the city. This practice gave the city a bad reputation; its vices and immorality humiliated all of the citizens. So, it was a serious offence to call someone Corinthian in those days.

The church at Corinth was comprised mainly of four groups of people; namely, Jewish converts from Judaism, former worshippers of Aphrodite, high-born rich Greeks, and some traders and travellers. This local church practically became an object of mockery and caricature because members of this assembly had dragged the name of the Lord to the dust. Many problems arose among the members, such as lack of unity and unstable leadership. Some of the leaders were sleeping with their fathers' wives. Taking one another to court was the order of the day. Other problems were marriage issues, immorality, issue of worship, the use of spiritual gifts, the matter of speaking in tongues, the Lord's Supper, the matter of the resurrection, and so many other problems. In order to address these difficulties, Apostle Paul was prompted to write his first letter to the Corinthians. Paul answered all the questions by the Word of God, and the situation was somehow arrested. With God's book—the Bible—every Church problem can be handled and solved.

The Book

Penman: Almost all scholars and early Church fathers with one voice agree without doubt that no other person than Apostle Paul was the writer. Clement of Rome, in AD 95, called the letter "the epistle of the blessed apostle Paul". Paul wrote the book.

Person (s) addressed: The Church at Corinth

Period covered: It was written from Ephesus (1 Corinthians 16:8, 19), perhaps between AD 54 and 55.

Position of the book in the Bible: Forty-sixth book

Purpose of the book: Paul's major reason for writing this book was to clearly explain to the assembly the right way of living as Christians. He explained how they should conduct themselves in God's house. He encouraged their faith and answered their long list of questions about several basic Christian beliefs.

Popular people in the book: Paul, Apollos, Corinthian Church brethren

Places in the book: Ephesus, Corinth

Particular events in the book: love is the foundation (1 Corinthians 13:1–13), the Jerusalem collection (1 Corinthians 16:1–4), faithful household (1 Corinthians 16:5–18), Paul's salutation (1 Corinthians 16:14–24).

Person of Christ in the book: The Last Adam (1 Corinthians 15:45), not the second Adam

Portrait of the book: Church epistle

The Contents

I. **The disorder in the Corinthian assembly** (1 Corinthians 1–4)

(a) Saints appreciated (1 Corinthians 1:1–9)

(b) Saints addressed (1 Corinthians 1:10–2:16)

(c) Saints advised (1 Corinthians 3:1–4:21)

II. **The difficulty in the Corinthian assembly** (1 Corinthians 5:1–15:58)

(a) Serious sins touched (1 Corinthians 5:1–6:20)

(b) Solid spiritual truth (1 Corinthians 7:1–14:40)

(c) Searching scriptures transforms (1 Corinthians 15:1–58)

III. **The desire of the apostle for the Corinthian assembly** (1 Corinthians 16)

(a) Collection plan for poor saints (1 Corinthians 16:1–4)

(b) Concerning Paul's plan for service (1 Corinthians 16:5–9)

(c) Closing with Paul's pithy salutation (1 Corinthians 16:10–24)

The Statistics

There are sixteen chapters in 1 Corinthians, 437 verses, and 9, 489 words.

Conclusion

The book of 1 Corinthians concludes that believers should come together in unity, love, and consideration for one another. As sincere seekers of the kingdom of heaven, we must stop offending God in our demeanour. God expects each of us to join hands with the ability given by the Holy Spirit to profit Christ's Body, the Church. Christians all over should live and tell the world that they belong to Christ, the Church's only head. Believers are members of the Church. Why all this fighting? One God, one Saviour, and one heaven!

2 Corinthians

Introduction

Having written to address the Corinthian church's problems while in Ephesus, Paul became anxious to find out how the Church members had reacted to his epistle. He left Ephesus for Troas where he anticipated to hearing from Titus. From there he crossed over to Macedonia (north of Greece). Titus met Apostle Paul there with mixed news. A little positive change had taken place, but there was yet an aggressive minority that was still opposed to the apostle. These intruders, who refused to repent of their wrongdoings, decided to question and challenge Paul's authority and apostleship. They came to the conclusion that Paul was a false apostle who was in the ministry for personal gain.

Apostle Paul, however, penned another letter, now known as the second book of Corinthians. In order to save the young Church immediately, in his letter, he thanked and praised God for the repentance of some Church members as well as the growth that had manifested. Then he defended his apostleship, providing full details of how he had been commissioned by the Lord, his numerous sufferings and experiences for the sake of his Lord, Christ. This second book was his response to the critics.

The Book

Penman: No reasonable scholar ever debates or denies the authorship of this book; Apostle Paul wrote it.

Person (s) addressed: The Corinthian Church

Period covered: It was written few months after the first book of 1 Corinthians, Probably AD 55.

Position of the book in the Bible: Forty-seventh book

Purpose of the book: Paul aimed to encourage the Church members for their changed lives and the progress in their faith since his initial letter. He answered his challengers and explained to them what they did not know previously. Apostle Paul also urged the Church to send money to the poor people in the Church in Jerusalem.

Popular people in the book: Paul, Titus

Places in the book: Macedonia, Corinth, Troas

Particular events in the book: new persons in Christ (2 Corinthians 5:11–21), Paul's difficulties (2 Corinthians 6:1–13), changed members (2 Corinthians 7:1–16), cheerful giving (2 Corinthians 8:1–15), Paul's defence (2 Corinthians 10:1–18), Paul and his critics (2 Corinthians 11:1–33), Paul's thorn (2 Corinthians 12:1–10), accredited as an apostle (2 Corinthians 12:11–12), Paul's advice and salutation (2 Corinthians 13:1–13).

Person of Christ in the book: Sin Bearer (2 Corinthians 5:18–19)

Portrait of the book: Church epistle

The Contents

I. **The great apostle's call** (2 Corinthians 1–5)

(a) His manner (2 Corinthians 1:1–2)

(b) His motives (2 Corinthians 1:3–2:17)

(c) His message (2 Corinthians 3:1–5:21)

II. **The great apostle's converts** (2 Corinthians 6–9)

(a) The boldness (2 Corinthians 6:1–7:16)

(b) The brother (2 Corinthians 8:1–24)

(c) The bounty (2 Corinthians 9:1–14)

III. **The great apostle's critics** (2 Corinthians 10–13)

(a) Attack on his appearance (2 Corinthians 10:1–18)

(b) Agility of his authority (2 Corinthians 11:1–13:10)

(c) Another of his appeal (2 Corinthians 13:11–14)

The Statistics

There are thirteen chapters in 2 Corinthians, 257 verses, and 6, 092 words.

Conclusion

It is worth studying 1 and 2 Corinthians. They are Church handbooks. A lot of individuals often preach from the first book while neglecting the second. Both should be studied and preached from because the books portray the glorious news that is the story of Jesus. Giving to the poor is encouraged in these books; respect for leadership is supported by Apostle Paul. Above all, we must all live as Christians and be what God wants us to be and live for His glory.

Galatians

Introduction

The book of Galatians is a book of freedom in Christ. Paul started a local assembly in Galatia on his first missionary tour. *Galatia*, *Celt*, and *Gaul* are all related terms. It may amaze you to know that a great number of people who speak English are of Celtic origin. That is to say, Apostle Paul at one time, wrote to their forefathers. In approximately 276 BC, many of these European Gauls went to live in what is today called Turkey. Their boundaries became fixed, and their state was named Galatia, a region of Asia Minor.

Shortly after the apostle's departure, some Jewish Christians arrived and told the new converts that Paul had wrongly taught them. These false teachers insisted that the people must follow and obey the laws of Moses even after salvation. Then they began immediately living contrary to what had been preached to them (Galatians 3:1). The teachers of Judaism were in the process of perverting Christ's Word; they also attacked the authority and credibility of Apostle Paul. In this regard, Paul wrote to defend the Gospel. He clearly declared he was a true apostle called by Christ, who was the end of the law. Paul refutes these zealots of the Mosaic Law.

The Book

Penman: Paul wrote this epistle, and there has never been a grave debate on this.

Person (s) addressed: The assembly of Galatians

Period covered: The Jerusalem council was presided over by Apostle James (Acts 15), and Paul's presence was very significant as decisions were reached concerning the plight of the Gentile believers. Besides, if the beloved apostle attended this crucial meeting after the writing of his letter to Galatians' Church, then the date of the book should be around AD 48.

Position of the book in the Bible: Forty-eighth book

Purpose of the book: The book aimed to correct errors of three group of people in the Galatians Church: (1) Jews who were converted to Christianity insist that their fellow Gentile believers should also obey the law of Moses. This was against the teachings of the New Testament Scripture, which is a standard in all matters of Church's life. (2) Those who embraced faith in Christ actually did not understand the true meaning of "liberty". There was abusive use of the term within. (3) Another sect said that Apostle Paul was nothing but a deceiver. For this reason, Paul addressed these individuals with proper approach and led them to good understanding. His purpose was to inform members of this local Church to completely depend on God instead on themselves.

Popular people in the book: Paul, Peter, James, John, Barnabas, Titus

Places in the book: Galatia, Jerusalem

Particular events in the book: law and faith (Galatians 3:1–14), no more slaves but children (Galatians 4:1–7), freedom in Christ (Galatians 5:1–5), works of the flesh (Galatians 5:19–21), fruit lists (Galatians 5:22–23), what one sows that he reaps (Galatians 6:7).

Person of Christ in the book: End of the Law (Galatians 3:13)

Portrait of the book: Doctrine

The Contents

I. **Paul's explanation of his authority** (Galatians 1–2)

(a) His reasons as servant of God (Galatians 1:1–10)

(b) His revelation reveals Son's grace (Galatians 1:11–24)

(c) His rebukes for sake of the Gospel (Galatians 2:1–21)

II. **Paul's exposition of his anchor** (Galatians 3–4)

(a) Galatians interrogated (Galatians 3:1–5)

(b) Grace introduced (Galatians 3:6–29)

(c) Gift inheritors (Galatians 4:1–31)

III. **Paul's exhortation for our advantages** (Galatians 5–6)

(a) The ruin of legalism without Christ (Galatians 5:1–15)

(b) The rule of likeness to Christ (Galatians 5:16–25)

(c) The law of life in Christ (Galatians 6:1–18)

The Statistics

There are six chapters in Galatians, 149 verses, and 3, 098 words.

Conclusion

Galatians was written in Antioch in Syria. Law keeps us bound whereas simple faith in Christ Jesus leads to freedom and endless life. God no longer remembers our sins when we come to his Son through repentance. So, no one buys eternal life; rather, we can have it freely. Moreover, the Heavenly Father never plays partiality at any time; he honours those who honour him. We must all allow God's Spirit to direct our lives. I am so glad salvation is not for sale. It is rechargeable. Anyone can have it.

Ephesians

Introduction

The book of Ephesians is a book of mystery because it contains truth never recorded before but now made known. Writing from his Roman prison without any particular problem in mind, Paul encouraged Ephesian believers, instructing and reminding them of the duties and opportunities they had as members of Christ's Body. While he was a prisoner in Rome, Paul wrote three other books; namely, Colossians, Philippians, and Philemon. These are known as the prison letters. His incarceration did not prevent him from being busy for his Lord. The Church at Ephesus (western Turkey) was giving a practical advice concerning how to live the Christian life (Ephesians 3:17; 4:21–22, 24; 5:2). It was a local congregation that upheld the truth of God's Word in its totality without compromise and hypocrisy but only later left her first love and was asked to restore that initial love.

The Book

Penman: Schleiermacher, a German-born liberal, has absolutely refused to acknowledge Paul as the author of Ephesians. Yet, the Scripture itself declares the apostle as its writer (Ephesians 1:1). We accept the witness of the Bible and absolutely discard any other opinion.

Person (s) addressed: The Church at Ephesus (Ephesians 1:1)

Period covered: Tychicus, co-worker in Christ, delivered this epistle to the congregation at Ephesus about AD 60–62 from Rome where Paul was in jail.

Position of the book in the Bible: Forty-ninth book

Purpose of the book: It intends to demonstrate that the "Church" Christ built was not just a building made with human hands as many assume today; it was made by individuals who had acknowledged Jesus as Lord and Saviour over their lives. They are everywhere and in different assemblies, though some good Bible-believing churches disagree with this notion. Anyway, the Scripture is a large library. Thank God for this Bible guide.

Popular people in the book: Paul, Tychicus

Places in the book: Ephesus, Rome

Particular events in the book: spiritual blessings (Ephesians 1:1–14), the apostle's prayer (Ephesians 1:15–23), dead but now alive (Ephesians 2:1–22), the mystery (Ephesians 3:1–13), gifts (Ephesians 4:1–16), good counsel for husband and wife (Ephesians 5:21–33), the armour of God (Ephesians 6:10–20).

Person of Christ in the book: Church's Head (Ephesians 5:23)

Portrait of the book: Church truth or doctrine

The Contents

I. **Christians' position in Christ** (Ephesians 1–3)

(a) Conqueror's undefeated saints (Ephesians 1:1–23)

(b) Common union of the saved (Ephesians 2:1–22)

(c) Committed unsearchable love of the Saviour (Ephesians 3:1–21)

II. **Christians' practical conduct** (Ephesians 4–5)

(a) Virtues in the body (Ephesians 4:1–32)

(b) Vitality of the believers (Ephesians 5:1–20)

(c) Vicarious benefits (Ephesians 5:21–33)

III. **Christians' proven consecration** (Ephesians 6)

(a) Peculiar admonition (Ephesians 6:1–9)

(b) Particular adversaries (Ephesians 6:10–12)

(c) Provided armours (Ephesians 6:13–24)

The Statistics

There are six chapters in Ephesians, 155 verses, and 3, 039 words.

Conclusion

Christians are meant to fight and win with their captain's assistance. They have all the necessary resources needed for the battle of life. Believers must be aware that Satan merely has wiles with which he tricks God's people, posing himself as a powerful being. Remember that the Lord of lords and King of kings, the only potentate, King Jesus, is on our side and still in control of his property (the world), which he created in his power and might. Since believers are one in Christ, they must work together in unity, proving to the world that they love their master, Jesus, by loving one another. They should never allow denominationalism to divide them. One in Christ!

Philippians

Introduction

Philippians is one of Apostle Paul's prison epistles. Irving Jensen is a renowned teacher of God's Word. In his book, *Simply Understanding the Bible*, he writes: "Philippi is often called the birth-place of European Christianity because the book of Acts records that the first believer in Europe was saved here" (Jensen 1990, 193). This convert was a woman. Philippi was about eight miles inland from Neapolis on the coast of Macedonia, northern Greece. The city was named after King Philip of Macedon.

Paul, in his second missionary trip, founded a local assembly of which the Philippian jailer was a member. Members of the Church visits Paul while he was in prison in Rome, bringing financial gifts and other things that helped him so dearly. In response to their kindness and care for him, Paul sent this "thank you letter" by the hand of Epaphroditus. This trusted messenger decided to stay with the apostle for a while, but unfortunately, he became seriously ill, even unto death.

In writing these letters, Paul expressed his trust in the people and then explained the problems he was going through. Setting before them the example of Christ's humility, he entreated them to imitate Christ's life in time of trials. Paul encouraged them to disallow anyone who opposed the genuine Gospel of Christ. He reminds them also to quickly settle disputes between two sisters, Euodia and Syntyche. We really don't know why they or couldn't tolerate each other.

The book of Philippians focuses on four basic words: *suffering*, *sacrifice*, *service*, and *sickness*. Apostle Paul wrote from prison as he suffered. Christ, the perfect example, sacrificed his life for the entire world. Timothy, one of the most faithful and trusted workers, exemplified service, and Epaphroditus became sick unto death. He did not count his life as anything because of the love of God in Christ. Paul recommended him. Finally, the apostle exhorts the people to live as citizens of heaven and keep applying and practicing all they had learned, heard, and seen him doing.

The Book

Penman: It was written by Apostle Paul.

Person (s) addressed: The Philippian church

Period covered: Circa AD 60–62

Position of the book in the Bible: Fiftieth book

Purpose of the book: Philippians was intended to demonstrate the apostle's sincere gratitude for the gifts he received from believers at Philippi. He reminded them that, though he was in captivity, the Gospel was not. He planned to visit if God was willing, and he hoped that the two women's disagreement should not continue or linger further.

Popular people in the book: Paul, Timothy, Luke, Epaphroditus

Places in the book: Philippi, Rome, Caesar's palace

Particular events in the book: citizens of heaven (Philippians 1:27–30), humility of Christ (Philippians 2:5–18), Epaphroditus (Philippians 2:25–29), the priceless gain (Philippians 3:1–11), last words and thanks (Philippians 4:1–23).

Person of Christ in the book: Believers Example (Philippians 2:5)

Portrait of the book: Personal letter

The Contents

I. **Triumphant experiences of Paul** (Philippians 1)

(a) Paul's praise and prayers (Philippians 1:1–11)

(b) Paul's purposes and prospects (phil. 1:12–26)

(c) Paul's plea and perseverance (Philippians 1:27–30)

II. **Tremendous examples of Paul** (Philippians 2)

(a) Christ sacrifice viewed (Philippians 2:1–18)

(b) Consecrated service verified (Philippians 2:19–24)

(c) Companion's sickness vindicated (Philippians 2:25–30)

III. **Tested exhortations of Paul** (Philippians 3–4)

(a) His prepared theology (Philippians 3:1–21)

(b) His positive thought (Philippians 4:1–9)

(c) His persistent thanksgiving (Philippians 4:10–23)

The Statistics

There are four chapters in Philippians, 104 verses, and 2, 002 words.

Conclusion

Paul never blamed God for his imprisonment; instead, he praised the Lord, prayed daily to him, and rejoiced in his hope. You are not in prison, yet you are not happy. Why? If you are a child of God, even in that situation, please rejoice! God is not ignorant of your circumstance. Rejoice in the Lord. Paul said, rejoice. I encourage you as well—please do rejoice. Cheer up! God is in control.

Colossians

Introduction

Colossae is a city in Asia Minor. It was an unimportant site during the Roman rule. The membership of the congregation was composed mainly of Gentile converts. The Epistle of Paul to Colossae was penned in response to the false teachings (heresies) that were brought to the attention of Paul. Epaphras was the man who initially ministered to this city about Christ. At the time of his letter, the apostle had never met the Church there proving he was not the planter. However, when the bad news got him, he reacted instantly. The dangerous and erroneous teachings that crept into the assembly came from a group of people who claimed to have more knowledge than anyone else, even the apostles. They denied the truth about the humanity of Christ. Another group followed Antinomianism, a belief that, since we are under the grace, we do not have to practice self-control but may give into or fulfil the desires of the body. The third group followed Judaism and believed that, in order for people to be right with God, they must follow a system of ceremonial observances. These cults threatened the life of the Church at Colossae. The final sects were those that believed that angels should be worshipped.

When we compare these beliefs with the Scripture, we can rapidly point out that they are deadly and poisonous. Paul completely refuted them in his letter because those arguments are empty philosophy that are absolutely groundless. He said that Christ is all we need.

The Book

Penman: The apostle Paul confirms he wrote the book (Colossians 1:1, 23; 4:18)

Person (s) addressed: The Church at Colossae

Period covered: About AD 60–62

Position of the book in the Bible: Fifty-first book

Purpose of the book: Its aim was to defend the Christian faith in the face of heresy that was threatening the entire community of faith at Colossae. It also aimed to inform those false teachers, enemies of the cross, that Jesus Christ is supreme over all who ever lived.

Popular people in the book: Paul, Epaphras, Onesimus, Tychicus, Aristarchus, Marcus, Justus, Barnabas, Luke, Demas, Archippus

Places in the book: Colossae, Rome

Particular events in the book: Christ's pre-eminence (Colossians 1:9–18), setting your mind on things above (Colossians 3:2), characteristics of a new man (Colossians 3:12–17), Christian home (Colossians 3:18–25), Christian exhortation (Colossians 4:16–18).

Person of Christ in the book: Preeminent One (Colossians 1:18)

Portrait of the book: Doctrine

The Contents

I. **The truth concerning Christ's pre-eminence** (Colossians 1)

(a) His deity as God (Colossians 1:1–19)

(b) His death as gateway (Colossians 1:20–22)

(c) His demands as genuine (Colossians 1:23–29)

II. **The truth concerning cults' presence** (Colossians 2)

(a) Experiencing the love (Colossians 2:1–7)

(b) Exposing the liars (Colossians 2:8)

(c) Exalting the Lord (Colossians 2:9–23)

III. **The truth concerning Christian life patterns** (Colossians 3–4)

(a) Basic standard for ambassadors (Colossians 3:1–17)

(b) Biblical steps for all (Colossians 3:18–4:6)

(c) Blissful speech for his associates (Colossians 4:7–18)

The Statistics

There are four chapters in Colossians, 95 verses, and 1, 998 words.

Conclusion

Colossians shows us how to live as children of God. Christ has shamed the devil, proving to the world that he rules the earth right now from the kingdom of heaven where he is sitting on the right hand of the Almighty God. The lordship of Jesus Christ is the total substructure of the Christian faith. God's power is sufficient, and he is the Lord of all. Jesus only should be worshipped. Finally, Apostle Paul clearly informs all in more detail concerning Christ and the cult, but the victorious Jesus, who is in control has amazingly given Christians authority to lead with him. That is good news! It is a truly non-negotiable fact of all times. Jesus is Lord.

1 Thessalonians

Introduction

If at any time you wish to study eschatology, the book of Thessalonians is the right one to begin with; it is the best of the books on the subject. In his second trip as successful missionary, Paul gathered a young congregation of believers made up of Jews and pagans. Among the pagans were many who already had joined Jewish religion known as Judaism.

After few months, Paul was forced out of the city by some leaders of the Jews (enemies of the Gospel) because he simply presented Jesus Christ as potentate and only Lord, not Emperor Caesar. So, Paul and Silas left for Athens and finally landed in Corinth where he wrote this letter. But at the end of his work there, he sent Timothy to visit the virgin Church to check on their progress and welfare. Timothy brought back a report that resulted in great relief mingled with a little confusion. However, while the believers remained steadfast and strong in their faith irrespective of severe persecution, they had no rest of mind about certain matters. They were unsettled about the condition of some believers among them who died before Jesus returns in glory. The apostle Paul answered these questions, seized the opportunity to express his sincere thanks for their steadfastness, and then encouraged them to maintain purity and have genuine respect for their spiritual leaders. He also advised them to have concern, care, and love for one another. He warned of certain moral dangers threatening them and advised that they should defend him against those unbelieving Jews who may come with another message about faith in Christ Jesus. He tenderly rebuked those who had stopped working in view of the coming of Christ.

Penman: Paul

Person (s) addressed: The Thessalonian church

Period covered: Written twenty years after the Saviour's departure to heaven, at Corinth about AD 50–51.

Position of the book in the bible: Fifty-second book

Purpose of the book: The letter intends to encourage the faithful believers not to give up the faith in the face of difficulties caused by the opposition by unbelieving Jews. He admonished them to live life pleasing to the Lord. He also writes to correct the misunderstanding about the return of Christ and urges them to defend the apostle's true concern for believers in Thessalonica against the intruders who attack his ministry.

Popular people in the book: Paul. Silas, Timothy, Jason

Places in the book: Thessalonica, Corinth, Berea, Athens

Particular events in the book: freed people (1 Thessalonians 1:2–10), persecuted but preserved (1 Thessalonians 2:1–16), Paul's desire to visit Thessalonica (1 Thessalonians 2:17–19), good report from Timothy (1 Thessalonians 3:1–13), things that are godly (1 Thessalonians 4:1–12), the Lord's coming (1 Thessalonians 4:13–16), concerned counsel (1 Thessalonians 5:12–25).

Person of Christ in the book: The Returning Lord (1 Thessalonians 4:16)

Portrait of the book: Church epistle

The Contents

I. The apostle's personal relationship with the church at Thessalonica (Thessalonians 1:1–3:13)

(a) Model church worshippers (1 Thessalonians 1:1–10)

(b) Message of Christ' worker (1 Thessalonians 2:1–20)

(c) Messenger's credible work (1 Thessalonians 3:1–13)

II. The apostle's protective revitalise words to the Church at Thessalonica (Thessalonians 4)

(a) Walk in purity (1 Thessalonians 4:1–7)

(b) Watch in love (1 Thessalonians 4:8–12)

(c) Wait in hope (1 Thessalonians 4:13–18)

III. The apostle's pious revivification truth to the Church at Thessalonica (Thessalonians 5)

(a) Paul's explanation of crucial truth (1 Thessalonians 5:1–11)

(b) Paul's exhortation of certified truth (1 Thessalonians 5:12–15)

(c) Paul's earnest request as central truth (1 Thessalonians 5:16–28)

The Statistics

There are five chapters in Thessalonians, 89 verses, and 1, 857 words.

Conclusion

The little letter of Apostle Paul contains important Christian doctrines; hence, the entire Scripture would have been incomplete without it, especially because of Paul's teachings about the coming of Christ. We understand the fact that one of the many themes of 1 Thessalonians is the coming of the Lord Jesus. Each of the five chapters deliberately mentions the coming of Christ. It might be the apostle's earliest epistle.

While we wait for Christ's return, McDonald references G. R. Harding Wood who came up with the following excellent synopsis: "The Christian who is expecting the return of the Lord Jesus Christ has no room for idols in his heart (1 Thessalonians 1:9, 10); slackness in his service (1 Thessalonians 2:9, 19); Divisions in his fellowship (1 Thessalonians 3:12, 13); Depression in his mind (1 Thessalonians 4:13–18); or sin in his life (1 Thessalonians 5:23)" (McDonald 1995, 2022). He is totally right. It would be something great if all believers add more effort today into announcing to the world the Saviour's arrival. Every child of God must take the opportunity as a privilege to proclaim him while there is time.

2 Thessalonians

Introduction

The second book of Paul to the saints at Thessalonica was written from Corinth shortly after his first letter, after just about a five-month interval. Either Apostle Paul's initial epistle or someone else's letter threw the recipients into more confusion, and this adds to the ongoing intense tribulation they were already experiencing. They misunderstood the doctrine presented, especially concerning the Lord's imminent return and the Day of the Lord. This automatically put them off the track. They lacked proper understanding and were confused by the message of false teachers. When the news got to the apostle, he did not hesitate in correcting them. He quickly wrote another letter assuring them that Christ's return would definitely bring joy and comfort, and that their persecutors would be severely punished. He encouraged those saints to endure suffering for the sake of Christ, while those living in idleness in view of the Lord's coming the second time were corrected. Some people today make same mistake made by this local assembly. They consider rapture to mean revelation without knowing that rapture has to do with secret while revelation deals with the public. However, there is a need for believers to study the Scriptures thoroughly in order to see the difference.

The Book

Penman: 2 Thessalonians 1:1; 3:17, together with some notable Church fathers like Polycarp, Ignatius, and Irenaeus accepted Paul as the writer of the book. Though many others have suggested one of Apostle Paul's associates such as Silas or Timothy as author. We will always believe the witness of the Bible.

Person (s) addressed: The saints at Thessalonica

Period covered: Since it was written just few months after the first letter while Paul, Silas, (Silvanus) and Timothy were still in Corinth in his second missionary journey, it was probably written between AD 50–51.

Position of the book in the Bible: Fifty-third book

Purpose of the book: The aim of this book was to stir up the faith of persecuted believers at the Church in Thessalonica, and at the same time, correct their wrong impression and views about the Day of the Lord because some had concluded it had already taken place so there was no more reason for their sufferings. Finally, Paul wrote to let them know they must work if they want to eat. We work as we wait for his appearing.

Popular people in the book: Paul, Silas, Timothy

Places in the book: Thessalonica

Particular events in the book: suffering brethren received words of comfort (2 Thessalonians 1:3–12), things you will see before his arrival (2 Thessalonians 2:1–12), hold tight the teachings (2 Thessalonians 2:13–17), pray for your leaders (2 Thessalonians 3:1–5), living the Christian life (2 Thessalonians 3:6–15).

Person of Christ in the book: The Coming Judge (2 Thessalonians 1:6)

Portrait of the book: Church doctrine

The Contents

I. **A word of encouragement** (2 Thessalonians 1)

(a) The Thessalonian saints (2 Thessalonians 1:1–2)

(b) The tried saints (2 Thessalonians 1:3–9)

(c) The triumphant saints (2 Thessalonians 1:10–12)

II. **A word of exhortation** (2 Thessalonians 2)

(a) Coming lie (2 Thessalonians 2:1–12)

(b) Chosen Lord (2 Thessalonians 2:13–15)

(c) Comforted love (2 Thessalonians 2:16–17)

III. **A word of edification** (2 Thessalonians 3)

(a) Petition of a lover (2 Thessalonians 3:1–5)

(b) Proper living (2 Thessalonians 3:6–15)

(c) Profound letter (2 Thessalonians 3:16–18)

The Statistics

There are three chapters in 2 Thessalonians, 47 verses, 1, 042 words.

Conclusion

Enduring persecution is part and parcel of the Christian faith. No believer runs away from suffering, and no believer should seek for it. One thing that comforts is that Christians are people with a future. Christ will fight for his own now and forever. Those who live without God now are in danger. Therefore, Christians should work hard, have enough for themselves, and be able to help others in need until Jesus comes again. Keep anticipating his return.

1 Timothy

Introduction

The book of 1 Timothy is the first book of the pastoral epistle written from Ephesus by Apostle Paul at the end of his ministry to his most trusted co-worker and labourer, Timothy of Derbe, who openly identified himself with the great apostle on his second missionary journey when he came to the city of Lystra in Galatia and also followed him on his third trip. Eunice, Timothy's mother, was Jewish born, but his father was a Greek Gentile believer.

Timothy was left by Paul in Ephesus with unhealthy situations that cause problems in the Church. His mentor asked him to give practical advice and instructions for carrying on the work of the congregation the right way. In his letter, Paul covered several topics such as Timothy's responsibilities, public worship, women's roles, prerequisites for leadership, and the duties of the Church in relation to poor people within the assembly.

The Book

Penman: Apostle Paul

Person (s) addressed: Young Pastor Timothy

Period covered: Approximately between AD 63 and 65

Position of the book in the Bible: Fifty-fourth book

Purpose of the book: The purpose of 1 Timothy was actually threefold: (1) Timothy, as a young minister, was having a hard time producing leaders in his assembly and needed help, so Paul wrote to encourage him not to quit in this service of the Lord even though it was tough. (2) False teaching was poisonous, and it divides and destroys Church's life. Paul informed Timothy about the presence of false teachers around, their method and how they operate. He told Timothy to fight and win. (3) Paul again intends to instruct his fellow worker how a church should be.

Popular people in the book: Paul, Timothy

Places in the book: Ephesus

Particular events in the book: warnings against heresies (1 Timothy 1:3–11), pastor Timothy's role (1 Timothy 1:18–20), instructions concerning worship (1 Timothy 2:1–15), elders' qualifications (1 Timothy 3:1–13), false teachers (4:1–5), good slaves (1 Timothy 4:6–16), practical advice in regard to categories of individuals in the local Church (1 Timothy 5:1–25), heresy and riches (6:3–10), useful instructions (1 Timothy 6:11–21).

Person of Christ in the book: The Mediator (1 Timothy 2:5)

Portrait of the book: Pastoral insight

The Contents

I. **A charge to Pastor Timothy relating to Church** (1 Timothy 1–3)

(a) Concerning the assembly's doctrine (1 Timothy 1:1–20)

(b) Concerning the assembly's devotions (1 Timothy 2:1–15)

(c) Concerning the assembly's duties (1 Timothy 3:1–16)

II. **A challenge to Pastor Timothy relating to Christians** (1 Timothy 4:1–6:10)

(a) The walk with God (1 Timothy 4:1–16)

(b) The witness for God (1 Timothy 5:1–6:2)

(c) The wholesome words of God (1 Timothy 6:3–10)

III. **A caution to Pastor Timothy relating to commitment** (1 Timothy 6:11–21)

(a) Follow what is right (1 Timothy 6:11)

(b) Fight with life in view (1 Timothy 6:12)

(c) Faithfully work to share (1 Timothy 6:12–21)

The Statistics

There are six chapters in 1 Timothy, 113 verses, and 2, 269 words.

Conclusion

False teachers should not be accommodated in the Christian congregation at any time. They can cause damage that could bring an end to a young local assembly if left unchecked. Right from the inception till now, God needs people who are sincere and honest to take over the leadership of his house. Good principles should guide the Church Christ owned. True possession is not about acquired wealth but in knowing what the will of God is in one's life as well as obeying and waiting upon God as he leads.

2 Timothy

Introduction

The Roman emperor, who perhaps died in AD 68, Nero by name, was hostile to Christians. He kindled the fire of persecution against Christ's disciples. It seems that Paul's second message to his beloved friend and associate, Timothy, created more of a stir than his first. His former imprisonment, as we know, had been light, but his imprisonment at the time of the second epistle was the one unto death. Paul was confined in Mamertine Prison. The only entrances to the cells were in the ceilings. Paul might have been put into the Tullianum, a dungeon known as the sepulchre. Here rats eat people alive. Many Christian friends forsake him, having seen the apostle's fate—the possibility of his death. Paul feels lonely (2 Timothy 1:15; 4:6, 9, 10, 16). Starting at the time of his conversion and carrying on until this period, Paul had demonstrated true love for God and his kingdom. His main concern was that Timothy should remain true to God in his service, irrespective of the inevitable difficulties caused by the heresy and persecution that encompassed him.

The Book

Penman: The apostle Paul wrote to his beloved and trusted fellow soldier in Christ, Timothy, while he was confined in the Mamertine Prison in Rome.

Person (s) addressed: Timothy, Paul's special friend

Period covered: Between AD 67 and 68

Position of the book in the Bible: Fifty-fifth book

Purpose of the book: Paul intends to encourage Timothy to be strong in his work for the Lord. He did not forget to pinpoint incoming trouble both in the assembly and in the world. Paul, at this time, desperately needs to have Timothy pay him a visit with something he was lacking there in prison (2 Timothy 4:13) and probably to see his dear son in faith for the last time before he dies (2 Timothy 4:6–8).

Popular people in the book: Paul; Timothy; Demas; Luke; Mark; Alexander, the coppersmith; Lois; Eunice; Onesiphorus; Janes; Jamnres; Trophimus

Places in the book: Rome

Particular events in the book: Timothy's mother and grandmother (2 Timothy 1:3–7), chosen and rejected workers (2 Timothy 2:14–26), dangerous period and dangerous people (2 Timothy 3:1–9), God's servant and God's Word (2 Timothy 3:10–17), Paul and loneliness (2 Timothy 4:9–16), the faithfulness of the Lord (2 Timothy 4:17–18).

Person of Christ in the book: Bestower of Crown (2 Timothy 4:8)

Portrait of the book: Pastoral insight

The Contents

I. **The command to protect the good news of Christ** (2 Timothy 1–2)

(a) His personal duties (2 Timothy 1:1–18)

(b) His pastoral dealings (2 Timothy 2:1–22)

(c) His perfect demands (2 Timothy 2:23–26)

II. **The command to preserve the good news of Christ** (2 Timothy 3)

(a) Description of apostasy and perversion (2 Timothy 3:1–9)

(b) Determined persecution (2 Timothy 3:10–13)

(c) Definitive persuasion (2 Timothy 3:14–17)

III. **The command to proclaim the good news of Christ** (2 Timothy 4)

(a) Paul's request (2 Timothy 4:1–5)

(b) Paul's reason (2 Timothy 4:6–8)

(c) Paul's refuge (2 Timothy 4:9–22)

The Statistics

There are four chapters in 2 Timothy, 83 verses, and 1, 703 words.

Conclusion

The beloved Apostle Paul was truly a spiritual father and mentor. He helped Timothy until his demise. Neither Paul nor Timothy was exempted from suffering for Christ's sake. Are you a true believer? Do you think you have faith? Are you sure of what you are saying? Be aware that your faith must be tested (2 Timothy 3:12). Expect persecution and insults because of your faith. Why should anyone be ashamed for being a follower of Jesus Christ? No one at all! All the truth believers must have to live for has been supplied in God's matchless Word, the Bible. Prepare to live for the Gospel and Christ.

Titus

Introduction

Titus was a young Gentile Christian missionary whom Paul sent to Corinth and Crete after his release from his initial Roman captivity. They both went to Crete, and Titus was left there to put things in order in the local assembly (Titus 1:5, 11, 13). Paul later needs his presence in Nicopolis. From there they journeyed to Dalamatia (2 Timothy 4:10). Titus was Paul's co-labourer who was really a competent and obedient follower of Jesus Christ.

The island of Crete is located in the eastern Mediterranean. There has been a speculation that the Cherethites, the bodyguards of King David, came from Crete, and it was the Philistines' homeland. In Acts, Luke informs readers that Paul stopped there on his trip to Rome as a prisoner. But the Cretans did not have good name among other nations. Some of them had become Christ's followers, and the apostle Paul desires the people to live as believers now they have believed (Titus 1:5, 12; 2:11–12).

The Book

Penman: Written by the beloved Apostle Paul.

Person (s) addressed: Titus, Paul's assistant

Period covered: The date of the book has been disputed, but obviously it was written between the writing of 1 Timothy and 2 Timothy not after 2 Timothy, perhaps A D 64–66

Position of the book in the Bible: Fifty-sixth book

Purpose of the book: The book intends to provide details to the young preacher Titus on how he should organise the local assembly which he supervised by carefully choosing its leaders. It was also intended to fight erroneous teachings within the Church and to encourage practical, holy living.

Popular people in the book: Paul, Titus, Artemas, Tychicus, Zenas

Places in the book: Crete, Nicopolis

Particular events in the book: God of all truth (Titus 1:1–4), qualified elders listed (Titus 1:5–16), a healthy congregation (Titus 2:1–10), the saving grace (Titus 2:11–15), inheritors of grace (Titus 3:1–8), know what to avoid (Titus 3:9–11), Paul's last message (Titus 3:12–15).

Person of Christ in the book: The Great Saviour (Titus 2:13)

Portrait of the book: Pastoral insight

The Contents

I. **The elders and errors in the local assembly** (Titus 1)

(a) Family and faithful men (Titus 1:1–9)

(b) False and faulty motives (Titus 1:10–13)

(c) Fake and fragile message (Titus 1:14–16)

II. **The exercise and examples of the local assembly** (Titus 2:1–3:11)

(a) Personal exercise (Titus 2:1–15)

(b) Practical exercise (Titus 3:1–10)

(c) Protective exercise (Titus 3:11)

III. **The epistle and exhortation to the local assembly** (Titus 3:12–15)

(a) The Apostle's genuine services (Titus 3:12)

(b) The Apostle's general suggestion (Titus 3:13–14)

(c) The Apostle's generous salutatory (Titus 3:15)

The Statistics

There are three chapters in Titus, 46 verses, and 921 words.

Conclusion

The Church should stand and refute wrong teachers and their wrong teachings. Paul never gives them a single chance; otherwise, the pollution of God's precious Word would certainly follow. The selection of people who should serve and lead in the Church is essential and must be done very carefully. Don't make anyone Church leader who is not qualified; otherwise, God's Spirit will be hindered.

Salvation is freely given to all people for this purpose. You need not struggle to have it; neither must you work to earn it. Moreover, good work is expected of all believers (Ephesians 2:10; Matthew 5:16). Every Christian should choose to live the way Christ lived and be willing to serve the great God and Saviour Jesus Christ, allowing his Spirit to transform him or her totally that others may see and thank God.

Philemon

Introduction

Philemon was a wealthy Christian brother from Colossae. His home was used for fellowship. His former slave, Onesimus, ran away to Rome where he met Paul, who was under house arrest at the time. Onesimus was led to Jesus Christ and became quite useful to the apostle as a young Christian convert. Now he became a believer, he consents with the apostle to go back to his owner, Philemon. When the decision was reached, Paul then wrote this personal letter appealing to his friend and convert to receive his former slave, who was now a fellow Christian, with love. Paul told Philemon to forgive Onesimus. He promised that whatever Onesimus had stolen would be paid back. Tychicus went along with Onesimus and delivered the letter. Do not forget that, in those days, slavery was an accepted practice in the Roman Empire. It was a business, and slaves were regarded as the owners' investments. As a result, a runaway slave was subject to capital punishment, and there were no chances for escaping the death penalty. That was the case with this man. But Christ in their lives make the difference. The New Testament Church neither attacks the practice nor did it supports it. More importantly, Paul paid Onesimus's debt just as Christ paid for our debt of sin on the cross. It is, of course, the doctrine of imputation. Martin Luther said, "We are all, the Lord's Onesimi." Paul was a mediator for the slave.

One of my university English lecturers said that the Bible supports slavery till now. But with my knowledge of Scriptures, I understand there is no specific support of it in the New Testament. So, I object to this notion because the practice may have been allowed in those periods for specific reasons and should not be used as standard. All men are created equal before God.

The Book

Penman: Paul wrote Philemon while he was under house arrest.

Person (s) addressed: Paul's convert and friend, Philemon

Period covered: This letter was sent to Philemon at the same time the letter to the church at Colossae was sent, between AD 60 and 62.

Position of the book in the Bible: Fifty-seventh book

Purpose of the book: Paul's sole aim in this book was to beg Philemon to forgive Onesimus and give him a second chance to be part of his family again—not as he used to be, but as a Christian brother who is equal with him and the rest of his household since both now serve the same Lord.

Popular people in the book: Paul, Philemon, Onesimus, Tychicus, Apphia, Archippus

Places in the book: Rome

Particular events in the book: From slave to saint (Philemon 16), a guest room (Philemon 22).

Person of Christ in the book: Father's Partner (Philemon 17)

Portrait of the book: Personal letter

The Contents

I. **Paul's praise of elder Philemon** (Philemon 1:1–7)

(a) The prisoner (Philemon 1:1–3)

(b) The prayers (Philemon 1:4–6)

(c) The partner (Philemon 1:7)

II. **Paul's plea for the new Christian, Onesimus** (Philemon 1:8–16)

(a) His request (Philemon 1:8–9)

(b) His reason (Philemon 1:10–12)

(c) His responsibility (Philemon 1:13–16)

III. **Paul's pledge as remarkable sign** (Philemon 1:17–25)

(a) Onesimus's enormous debt (Philemon 1:17–19)

(b) Philemon's assigned duty (Philemon 1:20–22)

(c) Paul's benediction and desire (Philemon 1:23–25)

The Statistics

There is only one chapter in Philemon, 25 verses, and 445 words.

Conclusion

This is the shortest epistle of Apostle Paul, but contains great lessons of love, courtesy, and the reality that should draw Christians' attention. If people are unable to forgive those who offend them when they seek forgiveness, they have not understood Christ and his work of redemption. Believers should pardon people who have wronged them in one way or the other, especially when asked to be forgiven. See others as you see yourself. We are brethren. The book of Philemon is small but beautiful and mighty in content.

Chapter 8

General Letters

The following books are known as general, universal, or catholic epistles. None of them is addressed to any specific individual or local church as were Pauline epistles; rather, they were addressed to all Christians or the universal Church. These include Hebrews, James, 1 Peter, 2 Peter, 1 John, 2 John, 3 John and Jude.

Hebrews

Introduction

Unless correctly touched by the Lord precisely, the old life will still show itself. These Jewish converts had been having second thoughts after leaving the Jewish religion for Christianity because of trials of faith. They were contemplating either returning to their former system and ways of living or remaining with unknown individuals most of whose leaders had been killed. It was absolutely a matter of leaving Judaism for Christ, shadows for substance, ritual for reality, temporal for permanence, and it was indeed leaving good for best. But this, they knew not. You may not understand why this was so serious.

Any Jewish man who left his forefathers' religion was seen as lost in darkness and must be punished either by denying the person his family inheritance or by the community publicly disgracing him, which might result in a jail sentence or even a death sentence. With this in view, there was always a way out. When the news of the shaking faith and an attempt to denounce Christ came to the ears of the author, he quickly points out why these people should not return to their old lifestyle. He told them that Jesus was superior to angels. Jews knew angels' special work in the history of their nation. Jesus was superior to Moses. Moses was highly regarded and respected. He was the lawgiver. Jesus was superior to Joshua, a powerful military commander who later became Israel's leader after Moses. Jesus was superior to Aaron. These people understood the glory of the Aaronic priesthood and the Old Testament priests. Christ's death was enough sacrifice.

The Hebrews writer, whomever he may be, stressed that a life of faith in Christ would be far better than their old lives since none of the great men I have just mentioned came near to comparing with Jesus. The author then encouraged them to fix their eyes on Jesus, who is the author and finisher of our faith (Hebrews 12:2).

The Book

Penman: The book does not clearly show us the author. Clement of Rome used the book of Hebrews in AD 95. It was said that Justin Martyr and Apostle John's deputy, Polycarp, quoted the same book without naming the writer. Dionysius of Alexandria quotes Hebrews as if it was written by Paul, while clement of Alexandria said Paul wrote it in the Hebrew language, and the physician Luke translated it. Irenaeus and Hippolytus did not believe it to be Paul's writing. Several names have been suggested as possible authors: Barnabas, Philip the evangelist, Luke, Paul, or Apollos. Origen said, "God alone knows". One thing is obvious: when guessing who the writer could have been, we must know that he was someone with a Jewish background who had a good understanding of Jewish Scripture. However, I am of opinion that Paul may have penned this book but decided to hide his identity. Theologians should stop fighting amongst themselves about who may have written it.

Person (s) addressed: Jewish believers living somewhere in the Roman province, perhaps in Rome. Tradition has it that the letter was penned from Alexandria, Egypt, in North Africa, where there was an enormous Jewish community.

Period covered: Approximately before AD 70

Position of the book in the Bible: Fifty-eighth book

Purpose of the book: The writer was concerned that these converts were in the process of denying Jesus Christ, only to return to their forefathers' religion. He used Jewish Scripture quotations and images to prove how Christianity was better than Judaism. He warns against such unprofitable concepts and plainly explained that Christ was superior in every way to what they'd had when they were under the Mosaic Law.

Popular people in the book: Jesus, the Son of the living God and humanity's only hope; Moses, the man who was faithful in God's house, who challenged the Egyptian pharaoh, and the man whose burial place was hidden from man.

Places in the book: Rome, Jerusalem

Particular events in the book: God's eternal Son (Hebrews 1:1–14), Jesus the Man (Hebrews 2:5–18), superiority of Christ (Hebrews 3:1–19), rest for God's community (Hebrews 4:1–13), our high priest (Hebrews 4:14–16), spiritual growth (Hebrews 5:11–14), Melchizedek and Abraham (Hebrews 7:1–17), old rule (Hebrews 9:1–10), our perfect example (Hebrews 9:11–28), one sacrifice (Hebrews 10:1–39), catalogues of heroes (Hebrews 11:1–40), all eyes on Jesus (Hebrews 12:1–13), a call (Hebrews 12:14–29), final moral instructions (Hebrews 13:1–25).

Person of Christ in the book: Law Fulfiller (Hebrews 10:7)

Portrait of the book: Doctrine

The Contents

I. **The supreme person of Christ** (Hebrews 1:1–8:13)

(a) His superiority in majesty (Hebrews 1:1–2:18)

(b) His superiority in ministry (Hebrews 3:1–8:5)

(c) His superiority in mediation (Hebrews 8:6–13)

II. **The sacrificial provisions of the cross** (Hebrews 9:1–10:18)

(a) A better sanctuary (Hebrews 9:1–13)

(b) A better sacrifice (Hebrews 9:14–10:9)

(c) A better sanctification (Hebrews 10:10–18)

III. **The sacred propositions of Christianity** (Hebrews 10:19–13:25)

(a) The warning and the emulation of faith (Hebrews 10:19–11:40)

 (b) The waiting and the exhortation of hope (Hebrews 12:1–29)

(c) The willingness and the extolling of love (Hebrews 13:1–25)

The Statistics

There are thirteen chapters in Hebrews 303 verses, and 6, 913 words.

Conclusion

The book of Hebrews is often called the fifth gospel because it chronicles the past work of Jesus while he was on earth and his present work in heaven. This book is significant and beautiful for its distinctive style and the logic by which information is presented.

Jesus is worth following especially when trials knock at the door, the mountains quake, and the billows. Just look unto him. If you ever doubt God's person, be assured of the following: One, Jesus is compassionate and perfect. He loves you and will always love you. Two, fellow Christians can be of great help to you. Just seek them for encouragement. They have or have had experienced the same circumstances you are experiencing. Three, there is strength in God's Word. Any good thing you need is in it. Dig and find treasures. In it you see yourself and everything about your Lord. The Bible contains all blessing that heaven has here on earth. That is true. Nothing untrue is added to this statement; rather, it is a simple truth. Test and see. Four, you don't have to suffer in silence; someone is there listening. With boldness, talk to God in prayer. Outline those problems to Him. Do you think he will not do something? He will. Five, do not stop seeing and watching the face of God.

James

Introduction

James in Greek is *Iakobos*. In Hebrew, the name is Yaakov or Jacob. It is a popular name among the Jews. Multiple individuals bore the name in Israel. To determine which of these four men really have this book, we shall examine each of them.

We have James, the son of Zebedee and Salome, brother of John the beloved, one of the twelve apostles, known as James the Great. Jesus called him and his brother, men of thunder. He was killed by Herod Agrippa around AD 44 (Matthew 4:21; 17:1; Mark 5:37; 10:35; Acts 1:11; 12:2). He died early before the writing of this book. He is the only apostle whose death is recorded in the New Testament, so he can't be the author.

Another James was the son of Alphaeus, one of the apostles. He was called James the Less or James the Younger (Mark 15:40; Matthew 10:3; Acts 1:13). Jerome appears to mix up this James with James, our Lord's brother. Still, he has identification and can't likely be the writer.

There is James, father of Judas (Luke 6:16). This man can be ruled out as possible writer because little is known of him.

The next James is the son of Mary and Joseph, half-brother of Jesus. He was very famous among the disciples, though he did not refer to his family relationship to the Lord Jesus Christ. This James later became leader of the Jerusalem Church and presided over the council. He was brutally stoned to death in AD 62 for refusing to denounce Christ. During Christ's earthly ministry, James did not know Christ as Lord and Saviour, but after his resurrection he became a disciple of Christ (Matthew 13:55; John 7:3–5; Acts 12:17; 1 Corinthians 15:7; Galatians 1:19; 2:9). He addressed himself in the opening verse as James. Of course, he does not need further identification as the author.

At the time of his letter, the Church consisted mainly Jewish Christians. That is why the content of his message had a lot to do with people in the Jewish community. James confronted them and accused them of being hearers of the Word of God without living it. He asked them to show their faith by their works and finally gave them some practical counsel for godly living.

The Book

Penman: James, the half-brother of Christ (Galatians 1:19)

Person (s) addressed: Jewish Christians throughout the Roman world

Period covered: The letter is directed to Jewish believers and might be one of the first New Testament books written. The outcome of the Jerusalem meeting (Acts 15) led by James was not mentioned in his letter, which could place its date between AD 45 and 48.

Position of the book in the Bible: Fifty-ninth book

Purpose of the book: Its aim was to let Jewish brethren know their lives did not fit what they professed to be. It also aimed to show how these people should practically put their faith to work. They were not maintaining love, showing mercy, or keeping their tongues under control.

Popular people in the book: James

Places in the book: No specific place or places mentioned—just nations where Christians were found.

Particular events in the book: trials profit (James 1:1–18), listen and do (James 1:19–27), prejudice condemned (James 2:1–13), when faith is not alive (James 2:14–26), lock your tongue inside (James 3:1–12), true wisdom (James 3:13–18), come near to god (James 4:1–10), judge no one (James 4:11–12), self-confidence can disappoint (James 4:13–17), the rich, patience in suffering, power of prayer, wandering brothers and sisters (James 5:1–20).

Person of Christ in the book: Lord of Glory (James 2:1)

Portrait of the book: Practical letter

The Contents

I. **The believer and his trials** (James 1–2)

(a) The Christians' battles (James 1:1–16)

(b) The Christians' Bible (James 1:17–27)

(c) The Christians' brethren (James 2:1–26)

II. **The believer and his testimony** (James 3:1–5:6)

(a) The Christians' behaviour (James 3:1–4:12)

(b) The Christians' boasting (James 4:13–17)

(c) The Christians' business (James 5:1–6)

III. **The believer and his triumph** (James 5:7–20)

(a) The Christians must be patient (James 5:7–12)

(b) The Christians must be prayerful (James 5:13–18)

(c) The Christians must be passionate (James 5:19–20)

The Statistics

There are five chapters in James, 108 verses, 2, 309 words.

Conclusion

Persecution and trials are evidence that we are not of the world. Rewards await as many as shall endure to the end. Faith and work are inseparable, and both are necessary. In the short note of James, Christians are instructed about the acceptable demeanour. Make it a policy to demonstrate your faith in Christ.

1 Peter

Introduction

Christ changed Simon's name. The Greek term *petros* and the Aramaic name Cephas both means "rock". Peter was one of the original twelve disciples. He suffered many pitfalls but never yielded to failure. He grew to be so profitable and an awesome witness and living warrior for his master, the Lord and Saviour Christ.

Believers throughout the Roman world were going through an organized kind of persecution. Perhaps what Nero began in Rome had extended to Asia Minor in present-day Turkey. The suffering of Christ's witnesses increased day by day, and conditions became unbearable. Peter was adversely affected. The persecution ended his life, but before his death in around AD 67 or 68, he wrote this letter to the saints who suffered for the sake of Christ. He emphasized that suffering was part of the Christian life. He used Christ as an example, whose steps believers must follow (1 Peter 2:2; 3:18–22).

The apostle encouraged the people to obey the government of Emperor Nero (1 Peter 2:13–17) and gave reasons for his advice (1 Peter 4:15–19). He concluded with exhortations to the shepherds with warnings concerning the devil. One thing that makes his epistle outstanding is the idea that sufferings and glory go hand in hand and cannot separate one from the other.

The Book

Penman: The former fisherman, son of Jonah, Apostle Peter

Person (s) addressed: Jewish and Gentile Christians in Asia Minor

Period covered: Since Emperor Nero's fierce persecution was in AD 64, the writing of 1 Peter was then between AD 64 and 65.

Position of the book in the Bible: Sixtieth book

Purpose of the book: Peter was writing to encourage believers who were suffering because they had placed their faith in Christ and were resolute in their plan to live godly lives for His sake, in spite of tribulations, until he returns from heaven for their reward.

Popular people in the book: Peter, Silas

Places in the book: Pontus (on the southern coast of the Black Sea), Galatia (central modern-day Turkey), Cappadocia (eastern modern-day Turkey), Asia (western modern-day Turkey), Bithynia (central northern modern-day Turkey)

Particular events in the book: the pilgrims (1 Peter, 1:1–2), hope of life (1 Peter 1:3–12), holy living required (1 Peter 1:13–25), obey the order (1 Peter 2:1–3), chosen group (1 Peter 2:4–10), allow them to speak good of God (1 Peter 2:11–12), respect authority (1 Peter 2:13–25), wives (1 Peter 3:1–6), husbands (1 Peter 3:7), inherit a blessing (1 Peter 3:8–12), our suffering and

Christ's (1 Peter 3:13–22), serving and suffering (1 Peter 4:1–19), submit and resist (1 Peter 5:1–11).

Person of Christ in the book: Theme of Old Testament Prophecy (1 Peter 2:7; Psalm 118:22)

Portrait of the book: Church epistle

The Contents

I. **Christians' position in Christ** (1 Peter 1:1–2:10)

(a) Consider their caller (1 Peter 1:1–12)

(b) Consider their conduct (1 Peter 1:13–2:3)

(c) Consider their chances (1 Peter 2:4–10)

II. **Christians' position in this cosmos** (1 Peter 2:11–3:22)

(a) Come out and comply (1 Peter 2:11–25)

(b) Couples and conditions (1 Peter 3:1–7)

(c) Courteous and conversation (1 Peter 3:8–22)

III. **Christians' position in the Church** (1 Peter 4–5)

(a) Saints and sufferings (1 Peter 4:1–19)

(b) Sheep and shepherds (1 Peter 5:1–7)

(c) Steadfast and salutation (1 Peter 5:8–14)

The Statistics

There are five chapters in 1 Peter, 105 verses, and 2, 482 words.

Conclusion

Expect suffering because of Christ; it is not strange to the Christian faith. You will experience God's glory in due time. Remember the popular slogan: No pain no gain. And, if there is no cross, there will be no crown. That is understandable. It is an opportunity for spiritual growth.

2 Peter

Introduction

The worst problems any family may have are the ones that are generated among the family members themselves. Outside disorders can easily be handled and resolved, but the ones inside are truly disturbing because they eat the family like a cancer. If you interview people who come from polygamous homes; they may verify this idea to your amazement.

Three years had gone by since Apostle Peter's first letter when he discovered that certain people had entered the assembly secretly. They pretend to be friends of the brethren, but they had the wrong idea about God's Word. They intend to subvert the true teaching of the Gospel and to turn the faith of the people away from the right doctrine, which had already received from Peter, whose journey on the earth at this stage was coming to a conclusion (2 Peter 1:14). Peter did not waste time to react to the urgent call. False teachers mocked the apostle's teaching about the Lord's coming. Peter, in his second letter, made them understand that God did not take joy in the death of sinners; rather he is patiently waiting and appealing to people everywhere to repent. He also urges Christians to grow in faith, creating awareness about the attack of the false teachers and advising the people to expect the return of Christ any moment now.

The Book

Penman: Scholars (like Origen, a Christian scholar of the third century) have been divided as to the authorship of the book. How could an ordinary person like Peter, who had little or no formal education, have written it (Acts 4:13)? But the opening verse of the letter suggests that Peter, the disciples' spokesman, was the true writer, possibly after writing his first epistle. Then he died.

Person (s) addressed: Jews and Gentile believers

Period covered: Peter was writing from Rome shortly before his demise, about AD 67.

Position of the book in the Bible: Sixty-first book

Purpose of the book: Peter realized he would not always communicate to these saints, and he decided to help them have true knowledge. He reminds Christians of all the things he had taught them. He also warned them about those secret men in their midst. Apostle Peter loaded them again with knowledge they could use to resist false teachers. He said that pure living must characterize their daily lives. The Lord must surely fulfil all his promises, he advised.

Popular people in the book: Peter

Places in the book: Rome, Sodom

Particular events in the book: precious faith (2 Peter 1:1–4), growing faith (2 Peter 1:5–11), prophecy of the epistle (2 Peter 1:12–21), false teachers' end (2 Peter 2:1–22), the day of the Lord (2 Peter 3:1–18).

Person of Christ in the book: The Long-Suffering Lord (2 Peter3:9)

Portrait of the book: Doctrine

The Contents

I. **The tasted knowledge of God** (2 Peter 1:1–21)

(a) A way of faith (2 Peter 1:1–2)

(b) A walk of faith (2 Peter 1:3–15)

(c) A word of faith (2 Peter 1:16–21)

II. **The twisted knowledge of the godless** (2 Peter 2:1–22)

(a) False teachers' doctrine (2 Peter 2:1–3)

(b) Fake teachers' destruction (2 Peter 2:3–9)

(c) Forge teachers' descriptions (2 Peter 2:10–22)

III. **The true knowledge of the Son's goal** (2 Peter 3:1–18)

(a) Scoffers exposed (2 Peter 3:1–7)

(b) Saints exhorted (2 Peter 3:8–16)

(c) Sobriety exonerated (2 Peter 3:17–18)

The Statistics

There are three chapters in 2 Peter, 61 verses, and 1, 559 words.

Conclusion

Christians are called to be holy and live to please the Lord, standing strong and refusing whatever opposes God's Word. Every wrongdoing has a negative reward. As to those who pervert the Bible in the name of knowledge, greater punishment awaits them. The Lord knows how to deliver his people. He knows the proper time to come. Don't worry about anything; only trust him and wait expectantly. All that causes pain, sorrow, and suffering will shortly be extinguished. There shall be a better new world made ready to be inhabited by God's true children. Just stay in him.

1 John

Introduction

John the beloved, an apostle of love, was the writer of five books in the Bible. He wrote to address assemblies that were in the process of being split by the enemies of the gospel known as Gnostics. The term *Gnosticism* is from the Greek word *gnosis*, which means "knowledge". This group support strange teaching about Jesus and held the idea that everything physical was corrupt and was totally evil. At this juncture, according to them, only knowledge—not Jesus Christ—saves.

They presumed that Christ died at the Gethsemane garden, but they believed that Jesus was ordinary man like any other person. They claimed that he couldn't be God and would not have come in human form if he is indeed the Godman that he claimed to be. These destroyers encourage people to sin with sweet talk in order to obtain their money.

John, therefore, wrote to fight deadly errors, to refute those antichrists in the Church. He then depicts believers meeting with God in fellowship as something of great comfort that brings joy, freed believers from moral laxity, guided them from falsehood, and impart eternal life through Jesus Christ. Never agree with heresy. The letter begins with no formal address. He assumes readers already recognise who the writer is. Notwithstanding, John was an eyewitness of what he penned. He did not debate with his opponents. He put down the truth on record for his generation and other generations.

The Book

Penman: Apostle John

Person (s) addressed: Church in Asia Minor (modern-day Turkey)

Period covered: John was old when he wrote the book, and close to the end of his life. He was at Ephesus, perhaps as the pastor of a church. This book was written late in the first century between AD 85 and 95.

Position of the book in the Bible: Sixty-second book

Purpose of the book: The aim is stated in the following passages: 1 John 1:4; 2:1, 7–8, 12–14, 21, 26; 5:13. John wants the people to grow into maturity as he praised their faith. According to him, a person is either a child of God or is completely the opposite. There is no middle ground. He disapproved of the activities of the false teachers. Finally, he wrote to give the assurance of eternal life—lasting joy—after this life.

Popular people in the book: John, false teachers

Places in the book: Ephesus

Particular events in the book: forgiveness possible (1 John 1: 1:1–10), believers barrister (1 John 2:1–14), antichrist (1 John 2:18–29), different children from different families (1 John 3:1–12), love your brother (1 John 3:13–21), prove of our love for God (1 John 4:1–21), assurance of salvation (1 John 5:1–20), avoid idolatry (1 John 5:21).

Person of Christ in the book: The Word of Life (1 John 1:1)

Portrait of the book: Doctrine

The Contents

I. **God is light** (1 John 1–2)

(a) Means of Christian fellowship (1 John 1:1–6)

(b) Marks of Christ's followers (1 John 1:7–2:14)

(c) Militants of communal faith (1 John 2:15–29)

II. **God is love** (1 John 3–4)

(a) Pure type of love (1 John 3:1–9)

(b) Practical tips of love (1 John 3:10–24)

(c) Perfect thought of love (1 John 4:1–21)

III. **God is life** (1 John 5)

(a) The received life (1 John 5:1–5)

(b) The recorded life (1 John 5:6–12)

(c) The revealed life (1 John 5:13–21)

The Statistics

There are five chapters in 1 John, 105 verses, and 2, 523 words.

Conclusion

Apostle Paul's characteristic words are *faith*, *hope*, and *love*, while Apostle John's are *light*, *love*, and *life*. John hereby presents Jesus as a true man and a true God against the concepts of false teachers. The apostle of love instructs believers to love other people as Christ has loved us. Keep away from idols. Christians should never be tempted to make God a spare tire.

2 John

Introduction

John was a dedicated and tested disciple who served his Lord to the end. It is said that, when he became too old, he was unable to preach and teach. He was then being carried to the congregation to offer them his words of wisdom. This may be why he used the phrase "my little children" so often in his first letter (1 John 2:1).

Early missionaries and teachers of God's Word would receive hospitality—things like food, money, valuable items, or other material things—in support of their labours from the believers whose homes and churches they visited. This was the practice in the early days. We read in the Scriptures that Jesus was a frequent guest of Mary, Martha, and Lazarus. Jesus at one time visits Peter's home and found his mother-in-law sick with a fever (Matthew 8:14–15; Mark 1:29–31; Luke 4:38–41). Many women also sponsored Christ's ministry, even with their substance. Unfortunately, false teachers immediately labelled this custom a means for making profit and, at the same time, pushing their wrong ideas about Christ and Christianity. John now let Christians know the need to keep their homes closed to those false teachers and to never partake of their evil works. Apostle John takes matter of heresy seriously (2 John 1:10–11). We must take a stand against it too.

The Book

Penman: Writing from Ephesus, Elder John addressed his letter to "the elect lady and her children". Likely this was the apostle's family friend, whom he had once met when she and her children were on a trip. John was extremely excited by their commitment to the Lord. Some have taken the elect lady and her children to be a particular assembly and its membership. Many Bible scholars believe the epistle addressed the elect lady Kyria, meaning that her name was Kyria, because Kyria is the Greek equivalent of the Aramaic name for Martha, which means "lady". However, that should not be a problem at all. One thing is certain, and that is that John appreciated the lovers of God.

Person (s) addressed: The elect lady and her children

Period covered: Circa AD 85–95

Position of the book in the Bible: Sixty-third book

Purpose of the book: John's epistle supports the practice of showing hospitality as it was in the early Church yet frowns at anyone who would welcome someone who was associated with teachers of erroneous doctrines. John's opinion is that we should always tell these teachers to show their back and then shut the door behind them. Preserve the faith, practice love, and avoid dishonest invaders.

Popular people in the book: Apostle John, the elect lady

Places in the book: Ephesus

Particular events in the book: the elder (2 John 1:1–3), living in truth (2 John 1:4–6), deceivers (2 John 1:7–11), elect lady's children (2 John 1:12–13).

Person of Christ in the book: Target of the Antichrist (2 John 1:7)

Portrait of the book: Family epistle

The Contents

I. **John's commendatory of the elect lady** (2 John 1:1–3)

(a) John's love (2 John 1:1–2)

(b) John's blessing (2 John 1:3)

(c) John's joy (2 John 1:4)

II. **John's commandment to the elect lady** (2 John 1:5–6)

(a) Test of faith (2 John 1:5a)

(b) Test of love (2 John 1:5b)

(c) Test of obedience (2 John 1:6)

III. **John's cautionary advice to the elect lady** (2 John 1:7–13)

(a) Awareness of deceivers (2 John 1:7–8)

(b) Abiding in doctrine (2 John 1:9–11)

(c) Audible, addressable, dissertation (2 John 1:12–13)

The Statistics

There is one chapter in 2 John, 13 verses, and 303 words.

Conclusion

Appreciating other Christians, especially when we know they walk with the Lord is permissible according to Scripture. Consider one another and show them love. Be able to elucidate what Jesus means to you to the critics. Some Christians have non-Christians as best friends. I do not contest that you should not have them, but make sure those friends don't spread and hold wrong concepts concerning Christ. Stay clear from anyone who poses as a threat to your faith.

3 John

Introduction

3 John is the shortest book in the New Testament. A glimpse of Church life in the first half of the first century is exposed in the characters of three prominent leaders in the Ephesians church— Gaius the hospitable, Demetrius the commendable, and Diotrephes the selfish.

John, in this epistle, commends Gaius for showing hospitality to missionaries, teachers, and the travelling evangelists who visit on their journey. Diotrephes, a power-hungry Church worker was condemned for chasing away true servants of God who came to the brethren as usual. He had expelled some members in his own authority for no just reason. And Demetrius was praised by the apostle for the good report he received about him. However, Apostle John sees Diotrephes' case as a problem to the Church's life; he intervened by writing this note in book form in order to handle and settle the matter. We must learn from the past and from the Bible.

The Book

Penman: See 1 John and 2 John

Person (s) addressed: Gaius, a committed believer from Derbe (Acts 20:4), who also is Church worker at Ephesus.

Period covered: See 1 John and 2 John

Position of the book in the Bible: Sixty-fourth book

Purpose of the book: John's major aim was to express his heartfelt commendation to Gaius for treating other Christian workers very well. He praised another worker in the Church for the excellent report received of him. And he confronted another leader of the assembly who always desired to be seen as overall supreme leader. So, outrightly, John warned against false teachers.

Popular people in the book: John, Gaius, Diotrephes, Demetrius

Places in the book: Ephesus

Particular events in the book: Gaius of Derbe recommended (3 John 1:5–8), Diotrephes condemned for wickedness (3 John 1:9–11), Demetrius praised (3 John 1:12).

Person of Christ in the book: Personification of Truth (3 John 1:3)

Portrait of the book: Personal epistle

The Contents

I. Gaius's prosperity recommended (3 John 1:1–8)

(a) His brave compliment (3 John 1:1)

(b) His bodily condition (3 John 1:2)

(c) His bold children (3 John 1:3–8)

II. **Diotrephes's pride renounced** (3 John 1:9–11)

(a) Assembly's selfish dictator (3 John 1:9)

(b) Antichrist's spirit denounced (3 John 1:10)

(c) Apostle's specific demand (3 John 1:11)

III. **Demetrius's report praised** (3 John 1:12–14)

(a) Reputation of good report (3 John 1:12)

(b) Reunion of glorious revelation (3 John 1:13)

(c) Remarkable greetings echoed (3 John 1:14)

The Statistics

There is one chapter in 3 John, 14 verses, and 299 words.

Conclusion

Gospel preachers feel joyful seeing members practice what they have been taught. We should demonstrate generous attitudes to all people, but we must sternly refuse to entertain those who do not teach and live the truth. Each member in God's house should protect his or her own heart, allowing only those things that bring growth and fruit in their work with the Lord God. Gaius was commended, Diotrephes was repudiated, and Demetrius received praise from John.

Jude

Introduction

Jude (Judas or Juda) was a common name in the New Testament. The Hebrew name is *Yehudah*. The short letter of Judah was written by Apostle James's brother, Jesus's own half-brother (Matthew 13:55; Mark 6:3; Acts 15:13–35; Galatians 1:19). Nothing much is said about him, but his little epistle has a loud voice and played a significant role in the Church's life then and still does now. Basically, his beautiful work bears a vehement similarity to the second book of Peter.

Upon hearing disturbing news concerning some who were going away from faith because of false teachers' deceit, Jude quickly appealed to believers not to participate in their sin. He wants them to understand the characteristics of the false teachers so that they could refuse them and remove them from the congregation. He also refers to Old Testament examples to caution believers of the judgment of God on those who did rebel against him in one way or the other.

The book contains graphic language of angels contending with the devil. Jude ends his letter with a glorious song of praise to God. Believers need to stand strong, fight, and win the battle over those who hate true gospel in the power of Christ alone.

The Book

Penman: Jude, a bondservant of Jesus Christ, and brother of James (Jude 1:1)

Person (s) addressed: Christians

Period covered: Written after 2 Peter was written, between AD 66 and 68.

Position of the book in the Bible: Sixty-fifth book

Purpose of the book: Jude planned to intimidate false teachers by exposing them and describing their final destructive destination

Popular people in the book: Jude

Places in the book: None mentioned

Particular events in the book: common salvation (Jude 1:1–4), Israel and angels (Jude 1:5–12), end of false believers (Jude 1:13–19), build yourself (Jude 1:20–23), song of praise (Jude 1:24–25).

Person of Christ in the book: Believers' Security (Jude 1:24–25)

Portrait of the book: Christian Church epistle

The Contents

I. **Apostle Jude explains undiluted facts** (Jude 1:1–4)

(a) Jude's salutation (Jude 1:1–2)

(b) Jude's subject (Jude 1:3)

(c) Jude's surprise (Jude 1:4)

II. **Apostle Jude exposes unbelievers' fate** (Jude 1:5–16)

(a) Comparison in conjunction with the past (Jude 1:5–7)

(b) Critical check on the present (Jude 1:8–13)

(c) Candid about a coming prophecy (Jude 1:14–16)

III. **Apostle Jude exhorts unbeatable flawless** (Jude 1:17–25)

(a) Remember God's Word (Jude 1:17–19)

(b) Rejoicing in God's love (Jude 1:20–23)

(c) Revealing God's power (Jude 1:24–25)

The Statistics

There is one chapter in Jude, with 25, verses, and 613 words.

Conclusion

False teachers are in many places. Some are in various Christian denominations; others are in non-Christian organizations. Many are even in schools as teachers and lecturers. The warning we have from the Word of God from the onset is that they should not be given any chance to operate. However, if you come across any of them, don't go near them or listen to them. They are traps and devourers of faith. Trust only Jesus continually! Truth has been explained, while false teachers are completely exposed. The set-apart people of God have been encouraged to stand for the faith once delivered unto them.

Chapter 9

The New Testament Prophetical Book

There is only one book of prophecy in the New Testament. It gives us a glimpse into the events of the past, present, and the future. Above all, it gives us assurance that God cares for his people even in their present trials. It is nice to know this. Cheer up.

Revelation

Introduction

Revelation in Greek is *apokalupsis*, while in Latin is *revelation*. It simply means "to uncover". John revealed the amazing person of the Lord Jesus Christ, his particular programmes, and enormous power. The major circles of persecution against the early Christians during the second half of the first century was engineered by Emperor Nero, a corrupt leader who wanted to cover up all of his atrocities of AD 64. In July of that year, he burnt an important document of the empire and put the blame on the followers of Jesus Christ. Peter's martyrdom took place around AD 67, but in about June of the next year, Nero commits suicide. Domitian came to power, a brother of General Titus, to whom Vespasian, his father, entrusted the siege of Jerusalem. Domitian reigned as emperor in circa AD 95. John was exiled to Isle of Patmos where he wrote the book of Revelation. Two other emperors, Nerva and Trajan, ruled. During the time of the first-year rule of Trajan, John returned to Ephesus where he died. He was the only apostle who died naturally according to tradition.

This book is an essential book of the Bible because it contains descriptions of events that will take place in the future. It is a book of prophecy. With this, Christians are encouraged to realize that God has plans for his people, and these plans will surely come to pass. It enables all children of God to establish proper priorities in their lives as they recollect that he needs to be here as a sojourner. In reality, the book of Revelation is all about the past, present, and future events.

The Book

Penman: John (Revelation 1:1, 4, 9; 22:8)

Person (s) addressed: Seven Churches of Asia Minor

Period covered: AD 95

Position of the book in the Bible: Sixty-sixth book

Purpose of the book: John wrote to bring to a conclusion the prophetic truth of the Scriptures, which had begun by the Old Testament prophets. He encourages suffering Christian churches to stand firm for Jesus who is alive and watches everything going on from the right hand of God. He warns against laxity and also exhorts those who wait for his appearing not to give up because his coming is at hand.

Popular people in the book: John, Jesus, Elders

Places in the book: Isle of Patmos

Particular events in the book: seven churches' letters (Revelation 1:1–20), seven churches (Revelation 2:1–22), universal church in heaven (Revelation 4:1–11), the slain lamb (Revelation 5:1–14), the beast market (Revelation 13:1–18), 144000 believers (Revelation 14:1–5), Book of Life (Revelation 20:11–15), a serious warning (Revelation 22:18–21).

Person of Christ in the book: King of kings and Lord of lords (Revelation 19:16)

Portrait of the book: Prophecy

The Contents

I. Person of Christ shown to the beloved John (Revelation 1–4)

(a) John as vicegerent of God's clemency Jussive vicegerent clarity (Revelation 1:1–3)

(b) John's vision of Christ (Revelation 1:4–20)

(c) Jesus's view of the Church (Revelation 2:1–5:14)

II. Programme of Christ shown to the behaved John (Revelation 6–20)

(a) Sorrows had begun (Revelation 6–11)

(b) Suffering from beasts (Revelation 12–18)

(c) Saviour's winning battle (Revelation 19–20)

III. Power of Christ shown to the beneficent John (Revelation 21–22)

(a) Holy City of God declared (Revelation 21:1–8)

(b) Holy City's gold described (Revelation 21:9–22:6)

(c) Holy City's grace documented (Revelation 22:7–21)

The Statistics

There are twenty-two chapters in Revelation, 404 verses, and 12, 000 words.

Conclusion

Apostle John elucidates his vision with a divine message that came to him directly from Christ to the churches mentioned in this book. He passed the information to his audience. He described what was going to take place in future; he describes events that will happen in the world until the end. The vision of John about Jesus should motivate every lover of God. It is interesting to know that our Saviour is alive and in control over the affairs of men. His programmes indicate that the future is secure for believers, and his power is a sure evidence that all Christians have lasting hope. Since Christ has good purpose for the Church and Christians in mind, we must continue trusting him so that we will enter into that eternal state when time comes. Come, Lord Jesus.

Author's Note

Have you been blessed through the reading of this book? If you have, please would you be willing to inform someone else so that this guide can assist him or her likewise? Do not hesitate to share your testimony in order that God will take the glory. Perhaps you want to order an additional copy or copies. Kindly contact the publisher or the author at this email address: jmjesus03@gmail.com or phone +353 1 6266550; +353 899607905.

Appendix 1

Bible Canons

A biblical canon is a group of books of Scriptures that are considered authoritative. We must state here that, in Judaism, there are twenty-four books that make up the sacred writing. Protestants have sixty-six books. Catholics have seventy-three books but see the Bible as the Church's book. Orthodox Christians have seventy-eight books. But for the sake of this work, I shall give attention to the Bible that consists of sixty-six books, not because it belongs to the reformers; instead, because of its canonicity.

The term *canon* comes from the Greek word *kanon*, denoting "a rule". When used in relation to God's Word, such as the "canon of Scripture", it carries the notion of a standard or a defined limit. Athanasius was one of the Church writers who first used the word *canon*. Canonization is the process of deciding which writings should be designated as real Scripture. Four basic tests or measures were put forward: One, the author must be a man of God—a prophet or an apostle. He must be known and respected as a genuine God-fearing individual (2 Peter 1:21). Two, the contents of his message must match with his life. It must edify the hearers. It must be life-giving and wholesome. The narrative must be historically and scientifically certain without errors (John 8:32; Hebrews 4:12; 1 Peter 1:23). Three, again, it must have acceptance—all of God's people must accept it. Jews must accept as well as the churches (Romans 3:1–2; Colossians 4:16). And lastly, four, it must have been inspired. It must bear God's authority: "thus says the Lord". It must not contain mistakes of any kind (2 Peter 1:1:21; 2 Timothy 3:16; 1 Corinthians 2:4).

The sixty-six books of the Bible have passed all these criteria. However, in 1546, at the Council of Trent, the apocryphal books were officially added. They are known as the second canon: deuterocanonical books by the Roman Catholic Church. Unfortunately, Reformers strongly exclude these non-canonical second Temple Bible books because they deemed them unfit.

Alister McGrath, in his book, *An Introduction to Christianity,* clearly states that a distinction was thus drawn between the "Old Testament" and the "Apocrypha": the former consists of works found in Hebrew Bible, while the latter consists of works found in the Greek and Latin Bibles, but not in the Hebrew Bible. While some reformers permit that apocryphal works were edifying reading, there was general acceptance that these works could not be used as the basis of doctrine. Medieval theologians joined with the Council of Trent and defined Old Testament as "those Old Testament works contained in the Greek and Latin Bibles," thus eliminating any distinction between the "Old Testament" and "Apocrypha Literatures" (McGrath 2000, 16). However, here Catholics differ from Protestants.

There are canonical terminologies that worth noting:

Homologoumena – These canonical books are accepted by all Christians. They are found both in Hebrew and Greek Scriptures.

Antilegomena – These are canonical books that are believed to be authentic by many Christians, but not all. The Old Testament Antilegomena includes: Song of Solomon, Ecclesiastes, Esther, Ezekiel and Proverbs 26:4–5. Eusebius gave this name to writings whose place in the New

Testament canon of Scripture was disputed. Among this group of writings, Eusebius distinguished two sunsets: those generally recognized as part of the canon, such as epistles of James, 2 and 3 John; and those actually not canonized at all (Stravinskas 1991, 78–79). Other New Testament books are 2 Peter, Jude, and Revelation.

Apocrypha – These non-canonical books are accepted by few, especially the Roman Catholic Church. The seven chosen are: Tobit (Tobias), Judith, Wisdom, Ecclesiasticus, 1 Maccabees, 2 Maccabees, and Baruch. It is needless to list the New Testament's Apocrypha books again.

Pseudepigrapha – These are absolutely a non-canonical book rejected by most individuals, mostly Christians. A few of these are: Enoch, Assumption of Moses, Book of Adam and Eve, Life of Asenath, Book of Noah, Magic books of Moses, Sibylline Oracle, Zadokite Fragment, The Story of Ahikar, Pirke Aboth, and Psalm 15I. There are also New Testament books—about twenty-one Gospels—including Andrew, Barnabas, Nicodemus, John the Theologian, Revelation of Peter, and others.

Appendix 2

The Gap

Before this important period of history began, the Old Testament prophets had completed their writings. Any book written during the period of silence was ignored and not considered as original or canonical. Perhaps Apocrypha books were penned at this time with no apparent authorship and may not have been quoted by Jesus in all his teachings. God in his great power has used various available people to minister to his people of Israel, commencing with Prophet Noah and continuing to the last prophet of the Old Testament, Malachi, who lived in 397 BC. Between the time of prophet Malachi and the arrival of John the Baptist, was a span of about four hundred years of silence. God did not speak to any prophet in the land of Israel, and the period is regarded as intertestamental period. However, during this period, Moses' law was properly given attention to by the Jews. The synagogue became a centre of Jewish religious life. Many different sects were founded everywhere, and their activities were diverse. God used the Babylonians to purify Israel of idolatry. Alexander the Great overcame Persia and made Greek an official language of the people. After his death in 323 BC, four of his generals divided the kingdom among themselves. The Greeks, however, ruled the land of Palestine. Syria was one of the seats of authority over Palestine.

But in the second century, a priest by the name of Mattathias, with his five sons, rebelled against a Syrian official who tried to enforce heathen sacrifice in Modein, northwest of Jerusalem, his own village. Mattathias decimated a renegade Jew who did offer sacrifice, slew the Syrian staff, and fled to the mountains with his children. Multitudes supported and joined him in the revolt; even after Mattathias's death, three of his sons carried on the revolt in succession. They were able to take back Jerusalem, cleanse the Temple, and restore worship. A feast to celebrate this victory today is known as Hanukkah. The Jewish State was established and lasted about a century. Unfortunately, in 63 BC, the Romans overpowered them.

Incidentally, while all of this was going on here on earth, God was very busy planning and preparing the appearing of the Great God, the potentate, His only begotten Son, Jesus Christ. No wonder he was not interested in talking to anyone throughout the four hundred years that elapsed. The Lord's first coming in the world in human flesh brought about the end of this special period, the four hundred years of silence.

Appendix 3

Quotes about the Bible

The New Testament is the very best book that ever was or ever will be known in the world.

—Charles Dickens, English writer (1812–1870)

That book, sir, is the rock on which our republic rests.

—Andrew Jackson, seventh president of the United States (1767–1845)

I am standing on the Word of God, 'tis full of life divine; God's Spirit lives in ev'ry word and moves in ev'ry line.

—E. M. Wadsworth, composer of "I Am Standing on the Word of God" (1910)

It is impossible to rightly govern the world without God and Bible.

—George Washington, first president of the United States (1732–1799)

I am busily engaged in the study of the Bible. I believe it is God's word because it finds me where I am. I believe the Bible is the best gift God has ever given to man. All the good of the Saviour of the world is communicated to us through the Book.

—Abraham Lincoln, sixteenth president of the United States (1809–1865)

A thorough understanding of the Bible is better than a college of education.

—Theodore Roosevelt, twenty-sixth president of the United States (1858–1919)

When you have read the Bible, you know it is the word of God, because it is the key to your heart, your own happiness, and your own duty.

—Woodrow Wilson, twenty-eighth president of the United States (1856–1924)

Of the many influences that have shaped the United States into a distinctive nation and people, none may be said to be more fundamental and enduring than the Bible.

—Ronald Reagan, fortieth president of the United States (1911–2004)

The gospel is not a book; it is a living being, with an action, a power, which invades everything that opposes its extension, behold! It is upon this table: This book, surpassing all others. I never omit to read it, and every day with some pleasure.

—Napoleon Bonaparte, French emperor (1769–1821)

Ignorance of the Scriptures is ignorance of Christ.

—Jerome, one of the Church Fathers (circa 342–420)

There is a book worth all other books which were ever printed.

—Patrick Henry, American revolutionary leader and orator (1736–1799)

I believe that the existence of the Bible is the greatest benefit to the human race. Any attempt to belittle it, I believe, is a crime against humanity.

—Immanuel Kant, German idealist philosopher (1724–1804)

Education is useless without the Bible.

—Daniel Webster, American politician and noted orator (1782–1852)

We account the Scriptures of God to be the most sublime philosophy. I find more sure marks of authenticity in the Bible than in any profane history whatsoever

—Isaac Newton, English mathematician and scientist (1642–172)

We must not build on the sands of an uncertain and ever-changing science … but upon the rock of inspired Scriptures.

—Sir Ambrose Flemming, British electrical engineer and inventor (1849–1945)

This book had to be written by one of three people: good men, bad men or God. It couldn't have been written by good men because they said it was inspired by the revelation of God. Good men don't lie and deceive. It couldn't have been written by bad men because bad men would not write something that would condemn themselves. It leaves only one conclusion. It was given by divine inspiration of God.

—John Wesley, British religious leader who founded Methodism (1703–1791)

It is impossible to enslave mentally or socially a Bible-reading people. The principles of the Bible are the groundwork of human freedom.

—Horace Greeley, American writer and politician (1811–1872)

The book of God's Word.

—Francis Bacon, English statesman and writer (1561–1626)

England has two books; the Bible and Shakespeare. England made Shakespeare, but the Bible made England.

—Victor Hugo, French writer (1802–1885)

All Scripture is God-breathed, and He doesn't waste His breath.

—Jim McCotter, primary founder of Great Commission
International (GCI), which later became Great Commission Churches (GCC) (born 1945 or
1946)

I prefer to believe those writers who get their throats cut for what they write.

—Pascal, French philosopher and mathematician,
developed the modern theory of probability (1623–1662)

Today man sees all his hopes and aspirations crumbling before him. He is perplexed and knows
not whither he is drifting. But he must realize that the Bible is his refuge, and the rallying point for
all humanity. It is here man will find the solution of his present difficulties and guidance for his
future action, and unless he accepts with clear conscience the Bible and its great message, he
cannot hope for salvation. For my part, I glory in the Bible.

-Haile Selassie I, Emperor of Ethiopia (1891–1975)

Bibliography

Benware, Paul. *Survey of the Old Testament: Revised*. Chicago: Moody Press, 1993.

Benware, Paul. *Survey of The New Testament,* Chicago: Moody Press, 1990.

Bowker, John. *The Complete Bible Handbook: An Illustrated Companion*. London: Dorling Kindersley, 1999.

Demaray, Donald. *Bible Study Source Book,* Grand Rapids, Michigan: Zondervan Publishing House, 1964.

Dicharry, Warren. C. M. *Human Authors of the New Testament, Volume 1, Mark, Matthew, and Luke*. London: St. Pauls Publishing, Worcester: 1991.

Fuentes, Antonio. *A Guide to The Bible*. Houston: Lumen Christi Press, 1985.

Harrington, Wilfrid. *A New Guide to Reading and Studying the Bible*. Dublin: Veritas Publications, 1982.

Jensen, Irving. *Simply Understanding the Bible*. Minneapolis, Minnesota: Billy Graham Evangelistic Association, 1990.

Jones, Alexander. *The Gospel According to St Mark: A Text and Commentary for Students*. Liverpool and London: Charles Birchall & Sons, 1963.

MacDonald, William, and Arthur Farstad. *Enjoy Your Bible: Practical Pointers to Make Your Bible Study a Pleasure*. Grand Rapid, MI: Gospel Folio Press, 1999.

MacDonald, William. *Believer's Bible Commentary*. Nashville, Tennessee: Thomas Nelson Publishers, 1995.

McGee, Vernon. J. *Briefing the Bible*. Los Angeles: Thru the Bible, 2017.

McGrath, Alister. *An Introduction to Christianity*. Malden, Massachusetts: Blackwell Publishers, 2000.

Philips, John. *Exploring the Scriptures: An Overview of the Bible from Genesis to Revelation*. Grand Rapids, Michigan: Kregel Publications, 2001.

Philips, John. *Bible Explorer's Guide*. New Jersey: Loizeaux Brothers, 1987.

Powell, Allan Mark. *What Are They Saying about Luke*. New Jersey: Paulist Press, 1989.

Rhymer, Joseph, and Anthony, Bullen. *Companion to the Good News*. London: Collins Clear–Type Press, 1971.

Stravinskas, Peter M. J. (Editor) *Our Sunday Visitor's Catholic Encyclopedia*. Huntington, Indiana: Our Sunday Visitor Publishing Division, 1991.

Thomas Nelson Publishers. *Every Catholic's Guide to the Sacred Scriptures*. Nashville, Tennessee: Thomas Nelson Publishers, 1990.

Ward, Maisie. *They Saw His Glory: An Introduction to the Gospels and Acts*. London: Sheed and Ward, 1956.

Wevers, John. *Ezekiel*. London: Thomas Nelson and Sons, 1976.

www.ingramcontent.com/pod-product-compliance
Lightning Source LLC
Chambersburg PA
CBHW021636120626
46545CB00002B/571